How could you do that?!

Also by Dr. Laura Schlessinger

Ten Stupid Things Women Do to Mess Up Their Lives

Ten Stupid Things Men Do to Mess Up Their Lives

How could you do that?!

The Abdication of Character, Courage, and Conscience

Dr. Laura Schlessinger

HarperPerennial
A Division of HarperCollins*Publishers*

A hardcover edition of this book was published in 1996 by HarperCollins Publishers.

HarperCollins books may be purchased for educational, business, or sales promotional use. For information please write: Special Markets Department, HarperCollins Publishers, Inc., 10 East 53rd Street, New York, NY 10022.

First HarperPerennial edition published 1997.

Designed by Nancy Singer

The Library of Congress has catalogued the hardcover edition as follows:

Schlessinger, Laura.
    How could you do that?! : the abdication of character, courage, and
conscience / Laura Schlessinger. — 1st ed.
      p. cm.
   ISBN 0-06-017307-6
   1. Ethics. 2. Conduct of life. 3. Character. 4. Courage. 5. Conscience.
I. Title.
BJ1521.S35   1996
170'.44—dc20   95-46266

ISBN 0-06-092806-9 (pbk.)

97 98 99 00 01 ❖/RRD 10 9 8 7 6 5 4 3 2 1

Contents

❧

Acknowledgments

I'll admit it. I slaved on this book by myself for most of a year. And that's after eighteen years of studying, teaching, counseling, and on-air work to give myself the insight and experience to be able to formulate these ideas and opinions. I thank myself for all that effort.

That effort had a tremendous amount of support and assistance. Barney Rodrigues, who helped expand my ability to organize the material in this book by showing me that the computer is quicker and cleaner than 3-x-5 cards; Carolyn Fireside, who read and challenged and suggested this manuscript into its final form (and with whom I shared many a dental horror story); Diane Reverand, my editor, who wields a mighty, and brilliant, red pencil (a wonderful person); Larry Metzler, the engineer of my radio program who provides me with dubs of essential calls (and who is dearer to me than any brother might ever have been); Carolyn Holt, who screens the calls on my radio program, giving me the best opportunities to challenge myself and be of service to others (we definitely are soul-sisters); all my friends and colleagues responsible for my radio program: John Shanahan, Alan Fuller, Carla Shell, Judy Cords, Geoff Rich, Ramona Rideout, David Landau, Ken Williams, and David Hall; all my callers and listeners who suffer with me through the agony and the ecstacy of becoming more fully human.

In a special category is my family: my husband, Lew Bishop, and son, Deryk, both of whom really go way out of their way to help me in what we see as a family mission.

It takes many leaves before a tree will be able to shade.

I don't wonder that so many people search blindly for the 'meaning of life.' What they don't seem to understand is that life does not have meaning through mere existence or acquisition or fun. The meaning of life is inherent in the connections we make to others through honor and obligation.

Laura Schlessinger, Ph.D.

Introduction

❧

Never esteem anything as of advantage to you
that will make you break your word or lose your
self-respect.

Marcus Aurelius

I know what you'd like. Be honest. Generally you'd like to get your own way, get whatever you want, get back at anyone whom you perceive as having crossed you, get your dreams and fantasies to come true right now, get ahead with less sacrifice and effort, and get away with murder (figuratively, I hope)—all without any consequences or regrets. Such power.

Sound heavenly? Think about it more. I believe that this selection of apparent goodies would be a welcome basket into hell. Can you really imagine enjoying a life without altruism, compassion, sacrifice, commitment, obligation, work, goals, cooperation, love, and companionship? That's just some of what you'd miss if you were capable of those powers. And think of what life would be like for you if others had those powers. Oh no!

Sounds awful, doesn't it? Yes, it does. But, do you realize how often you do try to create a life with one or more of those powers? If you're reacting with an immediate "Not me!"—think again. Think of all the times you've tried to cut life's corners, played helpless, taken without returning, told stories about others, threatened and hurt, lied and manipulated, used and discarded, disdained or ignored the welfare of others, sacrificed your obligation to someone else's needs for personal gain, sold out on a principle for money or fame . . . and so it goes.

The modern-day "out," or excuse for such behaviors, is generally psychological: "Considering my hurts, disappointments, and traumas, I can't be responsible for the havoc I wreak in the lives of others or the mess I've made of my own life." Oh puhleeese. Do you really believe that only those people graced with great genetics, perfect parentage, and ideal social conditions can and will behave with character, courage, and conscience? Do you really believe that laziness, gutlessness, and selfishness are products only of some form of psychoneurosis? Nonsense.

The path to solid, supportive, healthy relationships, self-respect, and a quality life starts with the usually painful decision to do the right thing. This is the book to get you on that path, and to keep you focused on those goals.

Those of you who listen to my radio program know I don't make a secret of what I consider the all-importance of ethical behavior. And I came to that conclusion by listening to your stories for almost two decades.

I began my radio talk-program career simultaneously with my training in Marriage, Family, and Child Therapy. My education as a psychotherapist focused on the dynamic (interpersonal pressures and challenges) and unconscious motivations (inner compulsive drives) for people's behaviors and for their problems in coping with life. The training didn't exactly say that people were not at all responsible for their condition, but it did emphasize that external situations and internal angst provided an almost inexorable force that became explanation, if not excuse, for all the inappropriate, self-defeating, even destructive behaviors that messed up their lives.

Consequently, my early on-air radio dialogues were directed toward providing insights concerning the origins of the caller's uncomfortable, frustrating, and sometimes downright scary predicaments. I actually got quite good at moving with the caller toward an understanding of how their unfinished developmental stages, unmet needs, experiences of loss and frustration, hurts and fears led to their present-day problems. You know, associations like: "Your father abandoned you at a young age and of course you'd be scared to trust men. That explains your promiscuity. Now that you know that . . . "

Neat package. Too neat. It worried me. First, I was bothered by the notion that just because an objectively bad experience happened, that it necessarily caused the person's present problems. Reality just wouldn't support that position. All people to whom that event occurred did not turn out with the same type or quality of life. I switched my thinking from cause-effect to possible influence—as I worried just how great a role blaming something in the past and reverence for victimhood was functioning to help people stay stuck.

Since all people are not similarly affected by similar life experiences, I factored into my reasoning the unique, basically genetic personality of each caller. If you question the genetic contribution, simply ask any parent of more than one child whether or not the personalities of their kids have been different from each other and relatively consistent from birth. Not everyone responds to the same threat or input with the same response; the reactions of individuals are not simple, predictable, knee-jerk responses.

Finally, it struck me that even profound anger, hurt, or fear do not merely trip-wire a specific reaction; human beings control and redirect emotions all the time, even override them with conscious determination—and often pay a considerable emotional price of pain to accomplish this noble task.

The bottom line is that, regardless of the facts of our past, notwithstanding our perceptions and beliefs about ourselves and lives based on that past, we can and must make decisions and take actions that require something more special about us as human beings than simple emotional reactions.

With this realization I began to develop a profound respect for the choices humans are capable of making under circumstances ranging from the apparently mundane (like the young woman not getting her "own way" in her relationship who decides to appreciate what she does have without diminishing it with regrets about what she doesn't have) to the deeply profound (like the man who finds out his old girlfriend is a single mother with his two-year-old daughter and makes the child's welfare his priority, sacrificing a new job, home, and current relationship to move close to and parent his child). Callers were teaching me about the tenacity of spirit and nobility of purpose with which people can choose to behave—where sacrifice and suffering are seen as part of the elevation of the soul in accomplishing something truly special: being human.

I don't take the issue of our humanity lightly. My B.S. and Ph.D. are in Biology and Human Physiology, respectively. I'm awed by the majesty and miracle of even single-celled creatures, much less the complex physiology and behavior of the evolutionary epitome of life on earth, Homo sapiens.

But, there is something that separates human beings from being too simply categorized as yet another animal, and that something is morality. Without morality, we are no more than termites seeking survival and gratification at every moment and at all costs. With morality we transcend instinct and simple equations of learned response.

More and more I began to see that the problems people

wanted to solve, resolve, or avoid in the first place need to be approached along the lines of right and wrong. This is anathema to much of the psychological establishment, among whom feelings reign supreme, values are relative, and where there is no judgment and little challenge. I started talking about honor, integrity, and ethics in tandem with the more traditional psychological approach and BANG!!! My radio program took off and became an international phenomenon, while purely psychology-oriented shows have more or less dropped by the wayside.

The basic premise of my radio program and books has been that, regardless of emotional angst or tremendous temptation, to be fully human and to benefit maximally from the life experience, you must get back to the 3 C's: Character, Courage, and Conscience.

I begin each hour of my program with "I've Got New Attitude," sung by Patti LaBelle, because it expresses my belief that it is attitude, infinitely more than circumstance, that determines the quality of life. Life is often quite tough, challenging us to choose between seemingly esoteric, intangible ideals and getting goodies or good vibes right now. You have character when you most often choose ideals.

I've often told my listeners that once an ant finds a crumb, it is instinctively driven to communicate to the other ants about the find and then help bring the food to the colony. The ant is not being good by bringing home the bacon, it is responding to an inner biological program. No choice involved. And where there is no choice, there is no morality. Humans can choose between selfishness (or survival) and generosity (or sacrifice). You have courage when you most often choose generosity.

I've also described that children learn very early which behaviors get parental smiles and which get parental frowns or spanks. At this early stage, right and wrong have only to do with reward and punishment. However, with maturity, you learn to respect the wisdom, protection, benefits, and promise of a moral life. You have conscience when you most often compel yourself to do what is right for its own sake.

I truly believe that we, as human beings, should wish to be loved and embraced for our character, respected and relied on for our courage, and trusted for our conscience.

This book is partly prophylactic in intent. My aim is to show you how an adherence to the 3 Cs can help you prevent personal and interpersonal problems and dilemmas. It is also true that the concepts and illustrative examples within this book can guide and direct you toward repairing and restoring your spirit, your relationships, and your life.

Now go take on the challenges of Character, Courage, and Conscience.

1

❦

Yeah, I Know . . . But . . .

(Where's Your Character?)

*The most important human endeavor is the
striving for morality in our actions. Our inner
balance, and even our very existence depends
on it. Only morality in our actions can give
beauty and dignity to our lives.*

Albert Einstein

The number one most typically asked question of me in any
radio, magazine, TV, or newspaper interview is: "What is the
number one most typically asked question on your internationally syndicated show?"

My answer is twofold. First, although there is no typical
specific question, there is a more general one, namely, "Now
that I've done all these things I shouldn't have done, how can I
avoid the consequences I knew, but denied, and just hoped
would not happen?"

That's the truth. While many callers' questions are about
contemplation and anticipation (i.e., "What could/should I do
about . . . ?"), the majority are attempts at retroactivity (i.e., "I

know I created a mess, but how can I make it all better, come out differently, or better still, make it go away?").

Second, the number one response to my reminders of cause and effect, common sense, values, ethics, morality, and fair play is: "Yeah, I know, but . . . "—and at that moment there occurs the abdication of character, courage, and conscience. The "but . . ." is followed by all sorts of attempts to indemnify the action under scrutiny, for example, through saying, "But . . . I was . . .

- unhappy
- confused
- frightened
- in love
- scared to risk
- uncomfortable
- feeling lonely
- feeling needy
- feeling anxious

(By the way, by using the word *feeling,* most people think they are now on sacred ground, since pop psych has elevated feelings from information to irresistible force.)

- carried away
- vulnerable
- unawares
- victimized

Victimization status is the modern promised land of absolution from personal responsibility. Nobody is acknowledged to have free will or responsibility anymore. Everyone is the product of causation (i.e., "Such 'n such happened to me and made me do that."). There are no longer individuals, just victims in groups. One such popular trend is "Adult Child of Some Kind of Parent or Situation."

You know the final excuse that really gets my hackles to full quivering attention? It's when callers protest that they are "only human." ONLY human? As if one's humanness were a blueprint for instinctive, reflexive reactions to situations, like the rest of the animal kingdom. I see being "human" as the unique opportunity to use our mind and will to act in ways that elevate us above the the animal kingdom.

A perfect illustration of these clashing definitions of humanity occurs in the classic film *The African Queen*. Humphrey Bogart as Charlie, the solitary sailor, tries to invoke the "only human" excuse when he attempts to explain his prior drunken evening by saying that it was, after all, only human nature. Katharine Hepburn as Rosie, the missionary, peers over her Bible and aptly retorts, "We were put on the earth to rise above nature."

And it is largely with the 3 C's that we accomplish that. The 3 C's are Character, Courage, and Conscience, without which we are merely gigantic ants instinctively filling out our biologically determined destiny.

While natural selection did shape our minds and feelings, there is something extra special about the human mind that leads us to be able, if not always willing, to take that extra step past some action that makes sense on only the basis of "survival of the fittest," or "survival of the me."

No doubt about it, self-advancement and self-indulgence are powerful innate drives for personal status and pleasure. Even the motivation for seemingly altruistic behaviors (such as letting people in line in front of you, and sharing food and other resources) can be found in the common sense of "I do for you because I can expect some reciprocal benefits in the future." Humans are social animals, therefore we all rely on the kindness of kin for survival to some extent. Yet, if all giving is simply motivated by the expectation of eventually getting, where does our special "humanness" come in?

Right here! Human beings can actually derive pleasure in the very act of resisting temptations, from not getting something, someone, or someplace the easy way. Also, it's profoundly satisfying to forgo immediate pleasures and benefit another person at some expense of the self, even if no one else knows you've done it, eliminating the investment concept of reciprocal altruism and restoring character to its rightful place in our lives.

CHARACTER: THE FIRST C

Yes indeed, human beings derive pleasure from having character, which I once heard defined as "What you are when no one else is looking." For humans, brute strength and stealth are not enough. We value reputation, respect, admiration, and the long-lasting happiness that comes from the sacrifice, pains, and efforts that go into forging character. In addition to the specific pleasure humans take directly from rising above the pull of selfish desires, we gain the acceptance and affection of others.

Peek-a-Boo, Now I Really See You

Tina, twenty-two, was married for six months when she and her husband went to dinner with three other couples. All the guys at the table had been at Jack's bachelor party and took this opportunity to tell tales of how he'd carried on that fateful night, including having oral sex with one of the entertainment-type women at the party. Tina had asked Jack before and after the event if there was going to be drinking, women, and sex. He said yes to the first, and no to the rest.

When I asked Tina, "So, what are you left with?" she replied sadly, "I know that he lied to me before and after the fact, and that he had intimate sex with a complete stranger. I now see him as having little character and believe that I cannot trust him to resist impulses. For the 'long haul' of marriage, I don't see how I can trust him and count on him. I'm seriously considering an annulment."

Tina now sees her husband as having little "character." What does this mean? It suggests that in the inner battle between the self (interest/indulgence) and the obligation toward others (fairness/sacrifice), she imagines he will lean toward self. Therefore, she judges she can't count on him to do the right thing or honor his commitments to others. In her eyes, and in all of ours, this makes him less reliable, therefore less valuable as a potential partner, mate, co-parent, and friend.

The call ended with Tina in a contemplative and sad mood. While she understood the philosophical implications of what her decision needed to be based upon, she did not draw a conclusion by the end of the call.

An assessment of your character is either a social invitation or a warning to others about you—or it should be. Just yesterday a co-worker told me that his friend had been offered a terrific job opportunity by a long-time acquaintance. In the course of wooing the friend, the acquaintance told him about the time he'd bought a piano with his credit card and had never been billed for it; he has a piano, and somebody else never got paid for it.

When my friend asked me what I thought that acquaintance should have done, I replied that of course he should pay the bill. I added that the friend should make sure he gets his compensation up-front because the acquaintance already telegraphed in advance that he was a getting-without-giving type.

When Do I Get Mine?

Integrity, honesty, and honor may not give immediate rewards or gratification, and they can be life-threatening (for example, being a whistle-blower or turning state's evidence). The absence of integrity, honesty, and honor do not always bring punishment or scorn, and can be life-aggrandizing (connivers and cheats often gain power and wealth). Therefore, morality must be its own reward. That's what my caller Tony and I grappled with.

Tony is twenty-nine, single, and his career is about to take off. All it requires is that he concentrate and focus his time, effort, and resources specifically on his goal. One problem: Almost two years ago his older sister and her husband died in an accident. Another of Tony's sisters took in the two children, now ten and thirteen. However, the woman didn't have the money and space to handle the additional responsibility, so they had all moved in with Tony.

"Look," Tony complained, "I feel sorry for them, I really do. But isn't it my turn at life? I have so much I want to accomplish and this is the time. I don't think I'm being selfish, just practical. What do you think?"

Instead of giving him my opinion, I asked him one question: "If I could project you fifteen years into the future and you could look back at this time in your life, what would you want to see yourself having done?"

Sighing deeply and choking back the tears, Tony replied, "Continue to help them."

Clearly, to resist the inner drive toward self-indulgence over character requires a value system that judges some behaviors as better than others—along with a specialty known as Courage.

COURAGE: THE SECOND C

Merely sustaining life is a vegetative state; people who lead such lives report experiencing unhappiness and boredom. Thoroughly living life requires initiative, risk-taking, sustained action against odds, sacrificing for ideals and for others, leaps of faith. People who lead such lives report being happy, hopeful, and exhilarated . . . even when they fail.

Courage is to life what broth is to soup. It is the very context that gives experiences, events, and opportunities a special richness, flavor, and meaning.

Courage is also what gives values vibrancy. So many people espouse values about sex, abortion, honesty, etc., until the dilemma is theirs. Then, because of their particular circumstances, selfish needs, and uncomfortable feelings, the values become optional.

Yeah, But . . . I'm Only Human

A recent caller, Gayle, thirty-one, and I tussled with this concept when she began her call by telling me she needed to let her mother know that at age nineteen she'd had an abortion as the result of carelessness in an uncommitted, sex-for-fun relationship.

"Gayle, why do you have to let her know that now?"

"Well, because my younger sister is in the same situation and I want to make it easier for my mother."

"Easier for your mother? Interesting. What's the one sentence you want her to understand that would make it easier for her? One sentence."

"I want her to understand we can make mistakes, that we're only human."

"Only human? That makes me want to toss up my lunch. You do what you feel like without forethought or responsibility and then you say, 'Oh, well, that's human.' I see human as something very special. I reserve 'that was very human' for something that was magnificent—like courage, altruism, artistry. Not just doing what you feel like, then say, 'Ah, gosh, only human!' So, I disagree with your basic tenet. Is that what you're going to tell your kids—don't think about right and wrong or consequences and responsibilities?"

"No, I won't tell them that."

"But, Gayle, that's what you want your mother to accept and understand and it is the wrong message."

Gayle's mother has two daughters who had unprotected sex in noncommitted relationships and will have aborted what for them is inconvenient tissue without contemplating that the tissue was a grandchild to their mother. I suggested to Gayle that knowing of the loss would probably hurt her mother, then proposed that her sister have her baby and put it up for adoption in a two-parent family. That way, the child would not have to pay the ultimate price for their mother's moment of pleasure, passion, fantasy, and obvious risk. "Why," I asked Gayle, "does this innocent have to die because you and your sister are 'only human'?"

I further suggested that if there were anything to say to her mother it ought to be apologies for the pain and hurt and loss because her daughters were operating on animal instinct instead of human responsibility. Admitting she hadn't looked at the situation from that point of view, Gayle signed off by saying, "Thank you." I replied, "I'm glad you gave me a chance."

CONSCIENCE: THE THIRD C

I believe too many people use "Okay, I made a mistake" (where the word *mistake* is used instead of the more honest "did wrong") or "But I'm only human," or "I'm not perfect!" as an escape clause out of a guilty conscience. Proof of the pudding, do people mostly say these before or after life has caught up with them? If it's before, I'll accept, as innocent error, an initial attempt to deal with life and others that is corrected when the self-centeredness or folly is recognized. If it's after, though, the speakers hope or believe they cannot nor should not be condemned, criticized, or judged. With these protective clauses they demand to be excused.

We wish to be excused because guilt (internal pain from the disappointment in self) and shame (public awareness of our transgressions with the threat of condemnation and punishment) are painful emotions, and so we go through verbal and psychological contortions of blame and rationalizations.

Conscience, however, is not just about avoiding those negatives. Conscience, our capacity to judge ourselves in moral terms and to conform to those standards and values that we make a part of our inner being, is also motivated by good feelings such as pride (in our fulfillment of goodness), compassion, empathy, love, and identification (seeing ourselves in others, thereby imagining how our actions would feel if directed onto us).

Human beings, not tightly programmed by instinct like lower animals, are charged with the seemingly overwhelming responsibility of making judgments and choosing between behaviors. We have responsibility because we have control. The metaphorical point of Adam and Eve leaving the Garden of Eden is that humans have the ability and the inescapable requirement of making choices. These decisions are made continuously: from parking in handicapped spaces to save yourself time and steps to justifying your lack of quantity time with your children and family by exalting quality time.

Thelma made my day, and drove home this point, with her fax:

The more I listen to you the more wrong I see I have been in most of my decisions; not because you, Dr. Laura, say so, but because I now see I have always done what I wanted and then justified my actions after the fact to myself and others. Thanks to you, things are beginning to make sense.

Beware the Pleasure Principle

Why does there seem to be such an inner struggle between the concepts of human as instinctive animal and human as an elevated being of choices? Simple. It's all about immediate gratification: pleasure. Conscience would appear to get in the way of that.

The pleasure principle of which I speak has to do mostly with our confusion between the concepts of "happiness" and of "pleasure." While a balance of both is a great formula for a satisfying life, the confusion between the two, and the emphasis on the latter, have been devastating to individuals as well as families, and inevitably, society.

Pleasure is a discrete and enjoyable experience: a sugar-covered donut, great sex, listening to music, a foot rub, watching an absorbing movie. As satisfying as pure pleasure is, it is also transitory and often quite superficial.

"Happiness," as Stan Cohen wrote in the *Los Angeles Times*,

is making steady, measurable, and observable progress in achieving the long-term goals that are a part of a lifetime plan. Happiness is rooted in some combination of the most basic desires for a good life that nearly every functional individual holds: to love and be loved; to successfully raise a family; to share ample quality time with friends and loved ones; to be enjoyably engaged in a gainful pursuit, one that fully employs and continuously expands one's skills, has purpose, earns fair recognition and provides rewards that are economically and/or emotionally satisfying; and to be a valued and respected member of one's community and society.

In this regard, pleasure is an event; happiness is a process. Pleasure is an end point; happiness is the journey. Pleasure is material; happiness is spiritual. Pleasure is self-involved; happiness is outer- and other-involved.

When individuals disregard the process of their lives and focus mostly on the seduction of the pleasurable moment, their self-centered actions often generate pain for others and destruction to their ultimate potential for self-esteem and personal achievement.

To this point, Carol B. faxed the following:

> **As I was sitting in church yesterday I learned the following: True happiness requires fidelity to a worthy purpose. Then I realized, Dr. Laura, that you must be the happiest person on earth. Forge on, woman!**

Missives like Carol's not only affirm my efforts but help keep me focused on the process (teaching/helping) versus the moment (ratings/time cues).

A Good Conscience Has Its Perks

In childhood, conscience is our internalized fear of losing our parents' love and support. In adulthood, it's something we impose upon ourselves in order to become complete human beings. There is seemingly no biological benefit to acting with conscience; if there were, only moral individuals would survive and procreate. Sadly, we know that's not true. The benefit of conscience is that you won't suffer guilt (private) or shame (public), and that by your own self-imposed definition, you are a moral human, a special kind of animal who takes unique pride in elevating him/herself above the termites.

This attitude is usually associated with religion and spirituality. Why do all religions have firm rules about behaviors? Just to cut into your fun? Just to control you? No, it is as a guide to help individuals in their "human" struggle between immediate self-gratification and the positioning of their behaviors in special circumstances, like reserving sex for a committed love relationship, which then elevates human sexuality above crickets and termites and other animals responding mindlessly to instinctive, built-in reproductive urges.

Twenty-one-year-old Mitch's call helped clarify this point: "A lot of my characteristics, a lot of my beliefs do not fit with a lot of the people I see and interact with every day. You know, people my age."

"Meaning that you are more or less what?" I asked.

"Traditional. What I wanted to ask you is this: I've been in three, to me, long-term relationships. Since I'm only twenty-one, long-term is a year to two years. And, in all three of those relationships I have been in love with the other person. Two of these relationships have been sexual. Um, I am not currently in a relationship, but I met somebody on the telephone about one month ago. I'm in Seattle, she's in Dallas. She is thirty-one. We get along well over the phone."

"Mitch, my friend, I'm glad you said 'over the phone,' because it's not real life, it's real fantasy."

"Right, I understand that, but [See?! Here's the "but" that erases every intelligent thought that came before!] I've planned a trip for me to visit her and to spend the week to see how well we get along. My question to you is that, based on my background, what do you think?"

"Wow—it is certainly tough to beat out a romantic fantasy with intellect here. If in real life people got together like this the divorce rate would be four times what it is now.

"Your basic thirty-one-year-old woman might want to rent you for a while, but it's unlikely that she'll buy. So, this is about excitement and an opportunity for pure sexual gratification. If you are talking about a traditional relationship where you have much in common in values and experience, where you are working toward family, and other common goals—this isn't likely to be the opportunity."

There is a thrill and a pull to something like this—that this might be the magic to give your life meaning, that you might feel more manly and grown-up—at least for now. This pull is so exquisitely powerful that rationality is put by the wayside as a trade-off (choice) for the "fun," for the "pleasure."

TRADITIONAL VALUES

Here's the key, though. Mitch says that he is a "traditional guy." The point of traditionalism is that it gives you rules and values that serve as bridges, to carry you over these kinds of temptations. Otherwise, there is absolutely no point to calling yourself traditional, unless you just want to give some illusion of superiority or maturity (definitely Mitch).

Traditional values imply the following: there are going to be exciting temptations toward which we will feel drawn; we then use time-honored rules of conduct, including everything from etiquette to morality, to get us through the moment without acquiescing to it, because we know that ultimately it is likely not in our best interest to succumb.

Free At Last . . . Are You Sure?

Since the Sixties, however, the mentality has been "To hell with traditional values. I want to feel what I want to feel and do what I want to do and damn the consequences!" Well, the consequences are usually emotional pain, diminished self-esteem, and the breaking down of barriers that ultimately make us feel less as well as lost. "Traditional" values have an important place in our lives and in society. Mitch used the term too lightly. It is easy to call yourself anything. The true measure of a label is its use. Espousing values is merely paying lip service, unless they are invoked in a time of challenge and temptation.

The sexual revolution screamed that sexual mores and behaviors were repressive and not responsive to the real, healthy sensuality and sexuality. And so began the dissociation of sexual behavior from anything more meaningful than "We feel like it, it feels good, so why not? Who is hurt?"

Some realities were either ignored or minimized. Female sexuality afforded multiple orgasms, all right, but a more typically feminine need for context was denigrated in this Brave New Unisex World. Consequently, many women were left feeling betrayed and abandoned by their recreational sex partners when the guys continually found new recreational sex partners. Women also typically overromanticize these liaisons in order to imbue the casual encounter with (synthetic) meaning. Their eventual disappointments dealt a mighty blow to their self-esteem. Also lost was the social expectation for men to see and treat women as special. I believe that the women who succumbed to the Pinocchio promises of the sexual revolution didn't free up their sexuality as much as they lost the sense of specialness of that act and their special contribution to the life process and social cohesion. Two consensual adults is not nearly as spiritually elevating as two consensual committed adults. And, double standard notwithstanding, the title "woman" used to mean much more than just genital determination.

Finally, regardless of birth control, pilot error and contraceptive failure led to unwanted pregnancies, hurling women and their children into single-parent poverty and the loss of the male parental figure in the home. This catapulted teenage sex into the danger zone: pregnancy, abortions, lack of education, poverty, sexually transmitted diseases including AIDS, and drugs, drinking, and violence through the loss of the intact family support system.

Freedom Is Only Half the Ticket

Immediate gratification, pleasure, is all about perpetual and irresponsible freedom. But freedom abused is freedom lost. We all clamor to be free at all times with all things. If we truly were free, for example, all traffic intersections would be festivals of blood and twisted metal, instead of civilized, organized thoroughfares with light signals dictating driving behaviors.

Freedom needs to be balanced with respect for others and the special awareness that both to others and to ourselves, we are what we do. And mindless freedom of the moment carries a heavy price tag. The following letter highlights real freedom:

> I am, by most of society's standards, totally square. I am 32 years old and happily married with two beautiful girls—ages 3 and 6. In my youth, I decided the dating, relationship, marriage process was so full of land mines that I was going to play by the rules. I am so glad I did. I dated, but never slept with a woman until I married my wife at age 25. My wife was 26 when we married and was a virgin. We have

never cheated on each other and have a home built on trust, commitment, friendship, mutual respect and a lot of love. Each year our marriage gets better and better and it was good to start with. I have no fear of AIDS or other venereal diseases, I have no flashbacks of other women to compare with my wife, no guilt, and no custody or marital messes. What freedom!

Some say luck, but I say it had a lot to do with right choices.

When I listen to your show I become so grateful that I followed the course I did. Some call it a traditional way, some call it God's way, but I know it is simply the right way.

Sincerely,
Berin G.

A Quality Life

A quality life requires the constant exercise of character, courage, and conscience. In the chapters that follow, the folly of attempting to ignore or circumvent the 3 C's is demonstrated in actual calls and letters. Read them, identify elements of yourself, and elevate yourself to being truly human.

Dear Dr. Schlessinger:

As a listener who cares not about your specific religious persuasion but about your wisdom, I thank you for your calling us all to become more than crickets. Keep up the good work.

A former cricket trying to
work my way up the food chain

And, finally, one last poem faxed to me by dozens of listeners:

> **Watch your thoughts; they become words.**
> **Watch your words; they become actions.**
> **Watch your actions; they become habits.**
> **Watch your habits; they become character.**
> **Watch your character; it becomes your destiny.**
>
> *Author unknown*

2

I Know It's Wrong . . .
But . . .

(Where's Your Conscience?)

It is the eternal struggle between these two principles—right and wrong—throughout the world. They are the two principles that have stood face to face from the beginning of time; and will ever continue to struggle.

Abraham Lincoln

In one of the *Star Trek* motion pictures, Spock sacrifices his life to save the ship and its crew. His last words with Captain Kirk, his dear friend, concern the importance of balancing the needs of the many with the needs of the one. Clearly, at that moment, Spock put the needs of the many in front of his own need to stay alive.

In the sequel, Kirk and his crew risk everything to find and resurrect Spock. They are successful, and at the film's conclusion, Kirk emphasizes to Spock that the needs of the one are important to the many, especially when the one is a beloved friend.

Both positions seem crazy. Knowingly bypassing instinctive self-preservation is crazy. Potentially sacrificing many lives in order to save only one is crazy. And yet . . .

THE ONE AND THE MANY

"If I am not for myself," asks the Jewish proverb, "who will be? But if I am only for myself, who am I?"

In contrast to all other creatures on earth, only humans measure themselves against ideals of motivation and action. We are elevated above all other creatures because we have a moral sense: a notion of right and wrong and a determination to bring significance to our lives beyond mere existence and survival, by actions that are selfless and generous.

Our animal instinct provides a powerful impetus toward both self-preservation and immediate gratification. We demonstrate our humanity by the value we give to behaviors that emphasize commitments over rights and a respect for our obligations to others. These actions are rewarded with affection, respect, lofty reputation, and long-lasting happiness.

Humans are the only creatures on earth who take pleasure in resisting temptation, easy and fast gratification, and constant pleasure seeking. We respect, admire, trust, and love those whose struggle between self-interest and commitment tilts toward the latter: commitment, honor, duty, compassion.

Since the Sixties, we've experienced a social blunting of our moral sense by not only failing to judge behaviors (especially our own) but also by allowing tremendous leeway for excuses. Ironically, excuses by their very existence betray an awareness and acceptance of right and wrong. Any pathetic explanation or justification of a behavior suggests that there has been some deviance from an expected and valued norm. A ban on judging others comes as a relief to those who tend to lack the courage to be appropriate, as well as to those who make too many compromises out of expedience and/or selfishness.

And here's where some of you may get uppity about the word *morals,* as if it were an abstract and rude intrusion into your rights as an individual. I suppose you could look at ethical rules and expectations of behavior as a means of rigidly controlling your personal expression. Still, to be truly enjoyed, individual freedoms must take place in some sort of organized context. For example, you're free to buy any car you want and can afford. But it would be childish, not to say disastrous, to extend that freedom to include parking wherever you feel like it or obeying traffic signals only when the mood stikes you.

We could call resisting morals and values a regression to childishness—notice that children are possessive and territorial, always looking out to make sure they are being treated fairly, as in: "You gave Johnny two cookies and I only got one!" Their focus is on the one, and the one is only themselves.

Children have distinct notions of right and wrong, but only with respect to their own well-being. But, because they wish to be loved and protected by parents and family and enjoy the company of and attachment to others, they develop a broader sphere of behaviors, which includes fairness to others, sympathy, compassion, sacrifice (sharing), etiquette, etc. Perhaps some of that evolves naturally, but I think that most of the knowledge and desire to care and sacrifice for others is taught and reinforced until it becomes a habit.

When the moral climate becomes overwhelmingly selective, permissive, and relativistic, moral habits fall by the wayside. The social aspects of human interactions suffer (drugs, violence, teen sex, non- and extramarital babies, etc.) and personal satisfaction declines (innumerable therapies for unhappiness, substance abuse, you name it).

FEELING GOOD *VS.* DOING GOOD

A listener's letter summed up my own thinking about social permissiveness by writing:

> As you have said on your program, one of the side effects of the plethora of rights movements is the idea that all behaviors or "life-styles" are equally deserving of toleration. The effect of this is that everything then becomes morally equivalent. The problem, of course, is that the results of all behaviors are not equally desirable in the real world. I suspect that one reason some people like to be so "tolerant" is that they don't like to consider the consequences of their behaviors, especially the long-term sociological implications. Freedom shouldn't have consequences, right? I have watched three of my daughter's friends decide that their boyfriends were jerks and bad husband/father material—after they had the baby.

There is a profound difference between doing what feels good right now and doing what you know to be morally correct right now. The former results in a temporary thrill (if you're lucky) but not in long-term positive feeling about oneself. The latter results in a temporary frustration (a tough challenge) and a long-term positive feeling about the self.

Oh, here I go again with that self-esteem issue, the

absence of which too many people blame for the cause of their weak or bad behaviors. Well, it really seems to me that too many folks want the body of Schwarzenegger without getting out of bed! The development of self-esteem, like muscles, depends on repetitive positive action.

Listen, after almost twenty years of call-in radio, I can tell you that the main thrust of too many lives is an overemphasis on feeling good instead of doing good. Being admired and respected by the self and others has taken a back seat to feeling good, or, at least, avoiding feeling bad. And, oh boy, the excuses some of you can come up with for doing so!

BUT . . . I'M SO CONFUSED

When we're confronted with an uncomfortable dilemma, we often retreat into confusion—as in not knowing your right hand from your left, ethically speaking. I don't buy it. I think we always know the right thing to do. The confusion comes from trying to reconcile what you know to be morally correct with what you want, while avoiding the messy and uncomfortable consequences of your behaviors.

My caller, Becky, was in a self-proclaimed whirlwind of confusion because she'd done something she knew was wrong, but did it anyway because it made her too immediately uncomfortable not to. When I asked her what this "wrong" was that she'd done, she said, "I let a man move in with me . . . with me and the kids."

"Becky, why is that wrong?" I challenged.

"Because I have three small children and it's bad role modeling. Also, he's probably not permanent, and he's not so good with kids. And I know I should be independent and that this is not really a healthy relationship."

"So you knew that letting him move in was wrong, but telling him not to would have been too uncomfortable? What more would have been too uncomfortable?"

(She retreats.) "Oh, I'm just so confused."

"This isn't about confusion, Becky, it's about laziness, desperation, not holding on to principles, and a lack of strength and courage. Now don't run away from me again with this confusion gimmick. Based on what you admitted to just a moment ago, what do you need to do?"

Becky responded hesitantly, "Become . . . independent . . ."

"And to do that you need to . . . "

"Rely on myself."

"And to do that you need to . . . "

"Tell him to go away."

"But then you'd be alone and you'd rather be dead with worms crawling in your ears."

"Yeah, I think so," Becky admitted, laughing.

The quality of a person's life is only as strong as their weaknesses ultimately dictate. Becky was making not being alone the most important determinant of her behavior—important enough to put aside her values. Becky knew what she had to do, but wasn't exercising her courage. I reassured her that calling me took courage. Now all she had to do was use that courage to follow through on what she knew was right for her and her children.

AND WHO TEACHES THE CHILDREN?

We expect adults to be clear on the benefits of suffering short term for the long-term payoffs. We expect adults to be role models for the children. We expect adults to teach value concepts by example and by explanation. If not, where do the children learn these lessons of conscience and courage to build character?

Matt, fourteen, learned by talking to me. Matt's mom had stopped talking to him since she walked in on him and his girlfriend getting dangerously close to "doing it." From my conversation with Matt, it seemed clear that she hadn't talked to him about many important life issues even before this incident.

I asked him to pick one from the following possible motivations for his wanting to have sex at age fourteen:

1. To make a baby and to become a father?
2. To express a deep and life-long love?
3. To express a marital commitment?
4. To look cool to his friends?

Matt owned up to number four. "Yes, I don't want them to think I'm a wuss. They're all doin' it."

"Matt, did you tell this girl she was just a 'warm place to put it' so that you would prove yourself not a wuss? Was she let in on her true role in your life?"

"No, of course not."

"Well, Matt, how would you feel about one of your buddies or some other guy using your sister or your mom just to prove he's cool?"

"I'd be very upset. I guess I didn't think about that. I guess I didn't really think about her at all," he admitted.

I have been disheartened by how many children have no idea as to why something is right or wrong. With respect to values, today's kids are getting either no information or garbage information; I don't consider being pointed toward the condom distribution center any direction about morals.

It is especially easy when talking to children to get across the practical aspects of morals and values. I tell children that these concepts are about avoiding getting caught, getting hurt, and getting someone else hurt. For example, with respect to sex: getting caught means pregnancy and herpes and other STDs; getting hurt means giving too much physical and emotional intimacy in what will likely be a short relationship; and getting someone else hurt means realizing that you've used someone like furniture just to have an experience to brag about.

Finally, to bring home to Matt the notion of how one makes special something normal and natural like sex, I used the analogy of his taking a baseball signed by Mickey Mantle out to play in the mud. While it's just a baseball, we imbue it with specialness by reserving it for conditions that show respect.

"Matt, we do the same with sex. Perhaps you could start a whole new brand of peer pressure: pushing the principle of not doing anything you don't feel proud of."

Whether child or adult, we all need something to grab on to when we conceive of letting go of the familiar—for example, give up the conformation to peer pressure for the feeling of personal pride that comes from doing things you know to be right and good.

YEAH, I'M RELIGIOUS, WHAT DOES THAT HAVE TO DO WITH ANYTHING?

I must admit I'm disheartened by how many adults don't seem to have a clue as to the meaning and value of morals. I asked one woman struggling with a dilemma what "moral" meant. Not particularly seeing how the moral issue might solve her problem, she resisted answering as though it just weren't relevant to our discussion. When pushed by me she said, "Moral means good." I told her that cheesecake was good; chocolate cheesecake was better, but that neither was particularly moral.

A man identifying himself immediately in our conversation as a born-again Christian, separated from his wife, having sex and living-in with another woman, called because his guilt was getting to him.

When I asked him why he thought his religion did not condone sex outside marriage, living together, affairs, etc., his response was simply that it was a "sin." Believe it or not, that was all the explanation he was able to come up with! Well, no one these days is worried about bolts of lightning and ever-lasting fire and brimstone, so calling the behavior a sin, in and of itself, just doesn't seem to impress. I am saddened that too many pulpits don't challenge the folk in the pews (lest attendance drop?) about their personal behaviors in the context of moral choices, which ultimately give dignity to fundamentally animal behaviors.

BUT . . . I'M REALLY NOT LIKE THAT

If I'm correct in saying that there is immediate gratification in not doing wrong (pride), and long-range benefits in not doing wrong (happiness), then why do people do wrong?

Frankly, there is some immediate gratification in doing wrong (desires gratified), and some long-range benefits in doing wrong (acquisition and the appearance of status). So, why should we do right?

Now we've reached the heart of the dilemma. In our internal conflict between morality (actions and motives that are judged worthy or good) and self-interest, we permit inner and outer forces to blunt our moral sense.

Corinne is grounded in that very spot. Hers is an incredible story, not because of the "details," but because of Corinne's seemingly genuine surprise at my using value judgments to explore the issues.

Corinne is an identical twin. Some years back, her married twin sister was having an affair with a married man. The affair ended, her sister stayed married, but he didn't. Corinne has now been seeing the man for about a year, with her in Canada and the man in the United States.

Her complaints were twofold: first, she sees him only every weekend and wishes it were more. Second, this is a bit of a scandal for her family—in the sense that it's like déjà vu all over again. Therefore, they are pressuring her to dump him or they will disown her.

I asked about his divorce and whether there were children. She related that he has three childen under the age of six.

Frankly, I was flabbergasted.

Sibling rivalry is a powerful force, yet to put aside any value assessment about his behavior and her contribution, for the sake of "getting her sister's guy," was horrifying to me even to contemplate.

I did ask her if it bothered her that he barely sees his three children under the age of six, since he spends the weekends with her. She seemed flustered and only focused in on her needs.

Bluntly, I told her that I was dismayed that this kind of man was considered a "worthy catch," that I was dismayed that any woman would bed a man who virtually abandoned his children, that I was dismayed that she would consider his significance as a "trophy" in the sibling rivalry competition more important than basic values.

She struggled against my attempts to infuse some reality into this situation. But finally she said, "Well, I didn't plan it this way." Excuse me?!! What kind of denial of responsibility is that? Did she wake up one morning in his bed by magic?

It is truly amazing how we can try to dissociate our behaviors from recognition of who we are. We are what we do, and that's that! There is nowhere to hide from yourself when your behaviors outline a lack of ethics or values, i.e., character. And, as with Corinne, no psychological aches and pains of "Mom loved you more" justifies the actions.

I just loved it when Corinne pleaded that her actions weren't in her character. Oh, really? So when she does good, it's in character, and when she does wrong, it's not? Nope, I don't think so.

I see this extended to women who claim they do wrong because (and here we go again) they have low self-esteem, whereas the male wrongdoers have low character. No sir, I won't buy it. We do wrong because in our inner battle, morality is lost to immediate self-interest. And the reward for that is a moment's thrill and potpourri of destructive consequences. Now what truly amazes me is how many people make that trade-off and then complain bitterly about the price! Danielle was suffering just that kind of resentment.

BUT . . . I WANT TO FEEL GOOD!

Danielle, twenty-four, was stunned. She'd been married less than three years and had had a four-month affair during the time she was the mother of a toddler. Why the affair? "There were pressures, and responsibilities and financial problems," she said. "Real life," I said. "Yeah, I guess so," she responded sadly, "and now he's left me and now I want to stay."

In the tug-of-war between her right to happiness and her commitments and obligations to her husband and son, she picked right to happiness, as though the real-life problems only burdened her, and not her spouse, and that the problems of life are cured with illicit sex.

What was interesting in particular was her comment, "I know now that it was wrong. So, why am I being punished?"

Friends, I'm here to tell you that just saying, "Yeah, I know it was wrong . . . now let's just let it go and get on with it," doesn't necessarily bring absolution. Her actions helped him decide that she was not the person to be going with when the going got tough. She was struggling with the "unreasonable"concept that she wasn't going to be afforded practice runs at doing this level of "wrong."

You see, it's not a simple matter of an "oopsie." When you choose wrong because it suits you right now, the message you give others is that when it suits you, you may likely do wrong again. You become a threat and liability to others. That's a pragmatic reason, outside of pride in morality, not to do wrong.

Please do focus in on the word *choose*. Ultimately, every action is the result of choice with intent—no matter how much you'd like to blame the devil for makin' you do it. And that's what others recognize and note about you.

Mike, forty-seven, realized that when he had trouble enjoying his ill-gotten gain. It had made him feel important to have a long-term female friend always come to him to cry about her husband or the many painful affairs she'd been having. But now that they're together sexually, and he has something to lose, he worries about her character. "I wonder if she has a character defect that she could do all that. I'm embarrassed to say it is a problem and I can't seem to put it behind me, as she has. It makes me not trust her. I guess guys have a double standard, huh?"

Actually, people in general have a kind of double standard.

You can be compassionate, nonjudgmental, and forgiving as long as the victim isn't you. When the victim might be you, there is a sudden realization of the importance of honor and trust, and then it all doesn't feel that good anymore.

Facing truths about yourself, another, or the situation can be very disappointing, upsetting, and feel most threatening. You won't feel good . . . for now. However, a more permanent and meaningful good feeling can only come from facing truths. It takes courage to weather the pain, being willing to wait for the promised better feeling. Anybody going in for a root canal must accept this truth, or dentists, not the Maytag repairmen, would be the loneliest people on earth.

Sadly, many folks choose not to believe, not to use their courage, and opt for a convenient detour, usually having to do with sex, the ultimate opiate and the typical detour. Here's but a few:

Kerry, thirty-three, the happily married mother of four who has recently begun taking night classes to increase her self-esteem, is hungry for her classmate's body (I guess that's easier than memorizing for exams). Kerry says she has felt lonely, alienated, unimportant, and unappreciated her whole life, and is living with a fellow with whom she had a fake wedding ceremony because, "This guy makes me feel good." (Too bad fantasies have the duration of a puff of smoke.) Deirdre, twenty, is constantly hoping that the older guy who beds her down once a month or so might actually love her (simplifying her search for an adult, meaningful life).

Each of us is what we do, not what someone else does with us sexually. Pride, dignity, emotional health, maturity, and accomplishments are results of your courageous journey. Morals and values remind you about useless and dangerous detours that threaten your journey. Heed them.

BUT . . . I WANNA LOOK GOOD

Each of us is what we do, not how we look, or nobody would admire Mother Teresa, considering her lack of mascara. Better that you should want to look good morally.

Carol, forty, claimed she wanted to "become who I really am after sixteen years of marriage. But I don't have a tidy little answer for those who ask me about why I got a divorce."

"Tell me why you divorced."

"Because he demanded things sexually that I didn't understand so I had an affair."

"So the problem you're having in not being able to neatly explain your divorce is that you're having trouble finding an explanation that doesn't make you look bad."

"Right. I agree."

"Well then, maybe what you need to say is that in the past your way of solving problems was to sedate yourself with extramarital sex, but that now you've grown to be willing to face things without sedation. This lets the new person in your life know that you accept responsibilities and that you are more ethical and courageous now. That's important for a prospective new partner to learn. The best way to look good is to acknowledge truths instead of making up a 'tidy little answer' in order to look good. It's much more important to be good."

And when you haven't been good, there is no time like the present to honor truth by not rewriting history to look good. None of that makes you good. And all of that sets you up for yet another fall.

No matter how much you try to jam lies or half-truths or nifty distortions into the truth jar, they just won't fit.

BUT . . . I DON'T WANT TO FACE "ME"

A popular alternative detour to rewriting history is simply erasing it.

That was the case with a caller who was getting married in a few months and wondered whether she would tell her fiancé about a two-year affair she'd had with another woman, who was a married mother at the time. Although the sexual part of the relationship was over (the other woman stayed in her marriage), the two remained friends. The caller's ex-lover was even going to be in the wedding party.

When I stated that it seemed she had some confusion about her sexual orientation, she defensively replied, "No, I'm a born-again Christian." I pointed out that not acting out on lesbian feelings because of religious convictions doesn't eliminate those feelings. The implication is one of self-control, for which I have incredible respect. But there's no religion in the world that can protect you from you. How could the caller be one hundred percent sure that her lesbianism wouldn't become an issue again some time in the future, when her marriage and family would be at stake?

Although she didn't want to tell her future husband about her past because she was afraid she might lose him, I urged the woman to go ahead and do it anyway. Telling her fiancé her secret might indeed threaten their relationship, but it seemed to me that the man had a right to be clear about something so integral to his future. "He might," I told her, "break it off. He might continue and give you both the time to see how things evolve or stabilize. Either way, you owe him the respect of letting him know what he could possibly end up facing. Otherwise, your personal fear of loss is depriving him of his right to choose. That's not love. It's selfishness."

There's no doubt that facing truths is often unpleasant because it forces you to do something (change is scary) or consciously do nothing (sit without hope). If you avoid truths with rationalizations galore, you protect yourself from the challenges of change, and you maintain some semblance of false hope. Too bad that you usually also end up doing wrong—to yourself or your community.

BUT . . . I DON'T WANNA FACE THAT TRUTH

It's just amazing how, when given a choice of uncomfortable truths about our lives, we'll inevitably go for the one that:

1. Pertains to the "other" person in our lives
2. Makes us victims
3. Gives us just cause to whine and moan
4. Seemingly gives us no options
5. Explains the pain in our lives
6. Explains the nonproductiveness of our lives
7. Puts responsibility for our happiness outside ourselves
8. Justifies our (ineffectual) behaviors of rage
9. Gives us perpetual cause for complaint

. . . and from which we wouldn't move.

A perfect example of the above is the call I took from Brett, thirty-one, and Sunny, twenty-one, who are unmarried live-ins. All would be idyllic (yeah, right), Sunny protested, if it weren't for the fact that Brett goes out drinking with his buddies and, without calling home, stays out late instead of coming home. His beef was that she was obviously too controlling: "I don't do it as often as she says."

I hit them head-on with the announcement that Brett has

a drinking problem. You'd have thought Brett would have been the first to deny. Wrong, it was Sunny with "Well, ohhh, it's not that bad. If he would just stop doing that stuff, everything would be fine."

"And," I retorted, "if it ever rained enough in the Sahara you could plant tomatoes."

When it was just an issue of hurt feelings, power tugs-of-war, promises, and make-ups, the situation was "just terrible." When I made it an issue of a drinking problem, suddenly the situation was "not that bad." Appropriately, alcoholism appears more dangerously difficult than petty bickering, where tears and nagging seem impotently appropriate. If she acknowledges he's got a drinking problem and has no commitment to behaving like a family man, then she probably ought to get up and go. At twenty-one, entering adulthood, it is too easy for young women to cop out to their obligations toward their own growth to maturity by getting enmeshed with the kind of guy who wants a whiny, weak, dependent female.

The conversation was successful. Sunny finally said, "Yeah, I know it's wrong to be living with him, especially the way he behaves, but I'd have to unravel what I thought was my life."

And build a new and healthier one, yes she will. This is where courage comes in. Instead of scrambling to reconstruct someone else's previously chewed toast, have the courage to make your own unique loaf of bread.

BUT . . . I DON'T WANT TO BE IN CHARGE OF MY LIFE

It might seem obvious that getting out of a bad emotional and ethical place is a good idea. When it means you have to "go it alone" (for a while, and then risk new relationships) or "go it in a way different from what you are most familiar or used to"(and learn to tolerate the discomfort of learning new skills), people start backpedaling. They either push help away or do not take advantage of possibilities because they are simply too afraid or too lazy.

This was the case with Rita, twenty-nine, whose husband frequently hit her in front of their two-year-old daughter. "He's never broken any bones or given me any bad bruises, but he hits me in front of my two-year-old daughter and it upsets me." No kidding!

Rita finally decided to do something about the abuse. She contacted the local project for abused women, where she was instructed to call the police, file a report, and go to a shelter with her daughter. When I asked her how many of those recommendations she'd followed, she told me a little sheepishly that she was living at home with her husband. "After all," she rationalized, "I have a child. And he only hits when he's angry."

That's when I abdicated clinical cool and said, "You know, Rita, you keep your daughter in a house where violence is both hanging in the air as a threat and then actually takes place. You set an example for your daughter in terms of what she can expect in a marriage and you teach her what behavior is appropriate from a husband as well as what a wife should do about it. Interesting preschool education, don't you think? And you're doing all of this because you don't take action."

Rita hastened to inform me that she had made a personal counseling appointment for some weeks hence, but if she thought that would calm me down, she was dead wrong. "I don't think it takes intensive psychotherapy to figure you ought to get out," I told her. "Or that you should demand he go to a battering man's workshop, or that you should file charges."

It was at this point that Rita admitted she'd hoped that therapy would somehow just make it all better so that she really didn't have to take charge. She was still detouring around taking assertive steps, hoping the monster within him would magically disappear.

Since I'm a psychotherapist, you're probably astounded that I didn't jump for joy when Rita announced she was going for treatment. But, you know, going to therapy is sometimes used to go into hiding from action. In therapy, you talk. This is an extremely useful tool in its place, but talk without appropriate action is strictly a pacifier.

No, I don't feel it's necessary to understand why you think a certain way or don't take a certain action even though you know rationally that it's necessary. Would you expect your children to have to master the principles of thermodynamics and biological reflexes before you warned them not to stick their hands in a fire? No, of course not.

Rita's self-esteem was not eliminated by his smacks; her self-esteem was never fully developed in the first place by the obligatory actions of courage. Weakness and evil are natural bedmates.

Just remember that your unwillingness to take a stand or take an action in the face of fear, longing, hope, and abject emotional pain will ultimately determine the quality of your life. You must decide that doing wrong or tolerating wrong is much worse than any fear or discomfort. In testimonial to that point is Alicia's letter:

> In listening to your program I have relearned the meaning of two very important words: Responsibility and Reality. I used to be the typical victim. I won't get into all that except to say that I used to think that all men took advantage of poor me, and that I

had nothing to do with it. Now I know (and the reality is I always knew) that we are all responsible for our own actions and/or behaviors. Why are there not more people who are as real, responsible, and unafraid to say things as you are? Why aren't there more therapists like you? I got more out of listening to your show than I got out of two years of therapy and one month in a mental hospital. Anyway, thank you so much for all you do, and please, keep up the good work.

Wow, it actually comes down to the courage and conviction to make what you intelligently know to be a right decision and follow through on it. That was Joe's issue.

BUT . . . I DON'T WANT TO BE ALONE

Joe, twenty-six, has been in a relationship for a year and a half. Just recently, his twenty-five-year-old partner has been saying that she doesn't know if she can go on in the future without having sex with other people.

"She wants her freedom to fool around?"

"Yeah, we discussed it this week and I said that if it is really this need she had . . . "

"Oh, puhleeese," I screamed as we both laughed. "One has a need to eat, breathe, drink water . . . there is no 'need' to screw everything that isn't already nailed down, please excuse the naughtiness. That's not a need, that's a desire. A need is life and death, a desire is something you just 'damn well wanna do and the hell with anybody else.'"

Joe, laughing, said, "I hear you."

"Joe, don't let her make it sound like it's some physiological requirement for existence, or psychological requirement without which she will become psychotic!"

"Right, well, I don't agree with it but she said . . . "

". . . that she wants to fool around and have you, Joe, say it's okay. She doesn't want to be monogamous or faithful, she wants to build an ego on how many guys she can get. You believe this is wrong behavior, Joe?"

"Yeah. My question is do I continue to try to support her and work through whatever she's working through in her head or do I say, 'See ya'?"

"Joe, 'See ya' sounds right to me. Let her know that when she's ready for a monogamous relationship to call you. Tell her that you want something of quality and someone of quality in your life. Let her know that if she is choosing to solve her emotional problems by sexually fooling around you feel bad for her, but that you don't want to pay any price for it."

Joe needed to learn that people must be held accountable for their choices. If you yearn so much not to be alone that you will not be discerning about who you spend time with, you're sinking to the same level as the person who's giving you grief.

Giving up on your values to hold on to somebody is truly a sin against the self. When the other person lets go of values in order to feel juiced up about life, get goodies without giving much back, have superficial feedback about being wanted or special, it's a terrible mistake to do the same thing. Nice people like Joe, who just want to get along, often interpret others' bad behavior and lack of ethics as an emotional problem that must be causing them pain and therefore merits empathy—and for which tolerance is a healing balm. In actuality, these souls are self-centered, immature, and/or morally bankrupt people who do exactly what they want, period. When they are tolerated, they are deprived even of the external motivation to change their ways: rejection.

However, this appropriate rejection reaction is often set aside while you're feverishly trying to avoid some other emotional pain. At twenty-five, Kathy was leaving her second marriage. The first ended because of physical battery, the second due to his drug use. "Kathy, let's do this step by step," I began. "At what point did you know that husband number one was violent and that husband number two was on drugs?"

"I guess before I married," was her surprising answer. I could only imagine that she must have been running away from some other pain to walk knowingly into these disasters. I was right: "My parents were divorced, my brother died. I was upset."

Her answer to afraid and upset was to walk through the first two doors available. Now, at twenty-five, she is single with three children from two attempts to bury her emotional pain.

Please note that I'm not minimizing the importance of the needs for personal security and comfort. They're natural and normal desires. My problem is when they serve as motivations for doing and tolerating wrong. You see, if we don't get these needs met in healthy ways, we dig ourselves into an ever deepening ethical hole. Nor am I dismissing the intensity of emotional pain, but it is astonishing to me how little tolerance comtemporary America has for enduring it.

This is where meditative or Eastern philosophies have a lot to offer. I've been a martial artist for many years now and have learned to tolerate physical pain and to focus and discipline myself when my emotional pain might lead me to stay in bed and whine. I was in physical therapy the other day for a shoulder strain and the therapist apologized for all the pain he was causing me. I was surprised to realize that while I was aware of the pain I was not focusing on it or attending to it in any defensive way. I just let it be and was there with it. I credit the martial arts training and my philosophical evolution for that ability, because my training has helped me focus beyond the pain—to the opportunity of gain.

Our society needs to be taught more about tolerating physical and emotional discomfort until we have a way to deal with it that truly serves us. Otherwise, we focus only on emotional hurt, not emotional health. And our exaggerated elevation in importance of emotional hurt provides us with a thousand or more excuses to take the ethical detour straight into demeaning, counterproductive, desperation-based dilemmas—and to stay there.

BUT . . . I WANT TO PLEASE

You want demeaning? I'll give you demeaning! One caller confessed that her boyfriend wanted her to dress in sexy lingerie and a raincoat, come to his office, and flash him. She thought this was wrong, but wanted to please him and called me to ask if his request were reasonable. I suggested that she find a guy who wanted her because she read Socrates, not because she was willing to degrade herself for his selfish jollies so he could prove to his buddies he had a woman who would do anything he wanted. If he didn't want her after she declined to do his bidding, so much the better! Being wanted for the wrong reasons is no blessing and certainly no compliment. And no real closeness comes from giving up one's pride and integrity to please and thereby keep someone.

Another caller suggested that her answer to a problematic marriage was to let her Indonesian husband send their three-year-old son to stay with his parents in Jakarta. Mind you, the boy had never been away from his mommy and daddy before and was absolutely miserable, but she said that her husband said that the boy was better off in Indonesia than being exposed to the constant bickering between her and her husband.

There was that pesky downside: "When I called him the other night he was crying that he wanted to come home. He said he missed me. I didn't know what to do."

"Frankly, Debbie, the answer to the question of the bickering and fighting impact on your son is to stop your bad behaviors, not ship him off to Indonesia or anywhere else. From his point of view, he's been abandoned and rejected."

While the caller continued to rationalize that she was making the ultimate sacrifice for her son, she was really making it for her man, whom she had to please in order to keep from losing him. "But you're not afraid of losing yourself or your son," I suggested, to which she responded, "Ouch!"

Unfortunately, this dilemma of the children versus the man rears its ugly head much too often, as some women allow their children to observe as well as be personally victimized by their mate's pathological need to be alone.

The first day my counseling office was open I received a call from a young woman with two small children and a new boyfriend. "He wants me, but he doesn't want my kids. What should I do?" was her question. I couldn't believe anyone could even have a moment's confusion. I cannot fathom the choice being other than the children. Then I am confronted with a Susan Smith, who allegedly chose drowning her children because her boyfriend wasn't interested in quite that intense a family commitment.

In Larry Meeks's column in the *Los Angeles Daily News*, Ethnically Speaking, came the following letter:

> I am crying with sorrow and frustration over the letter from the woman whose friend is going to give up her five-year-old boy for adoption because her new husband cannot reconcile having a Mexican

stepson. I am a white woman with a Latino husband. We have a happy son who is satisfied with his cultural and racial heritage. Our son is living proof that "mixed" children are the best kind. If this ignorant, bigoted man and his weak-willed wife cannot appreciate the gift with which God has blessed them, I feel sorry for them. My husband and I would be more than delighted to open our home to this child. We would like to be considered as applicants for the boy's adoption.

Human beings thrive on attachment. And, like the examples above, some human beings don't want to have to choose between attachments. I guess they just want to grab and hang on for dear life. Unfortunately, with that attitude life doesn't stay dear.

BUT . . . I DON'T WANT TO BE ODD MAN OUT

Choices in objects of attachment must be made, since not all possibilities are healthy or workable. Choices need to be out of courage, because there is always something to lose we don't want to have to give up. And sometimes we just stand by our ethics and honor and let others choose whether or not to deal with us.

Monique's new seven-week-old baby, Briana, is going to be christened. Monique has to figure out who to "reject," her brother, who after a sex-change operation is now her sister, or her dad, who just won't deal with the whole thing.

Right now, Monique's brother Alex is the odd man out and Monique doesn't want to be ostracized with him. She doesn't want to hurt her brother or father.

My comments to her centered on the philosophical and spiritual aspects of religion and religious behaviors. Was the christening just an excuse for a party or the solemn introduction of this small child into a meaningful faith? If it is the latter, then mustn't Monique think beyond the party into the morality of her father's behavior and her response to it?

While one could expect and understand the family's confusion, hurt and upset over such a radical event as a sex-change operation, one does not have to accept this punishing, family-divisive and destructive behavior. I told Monique that her father's behavior was wrong, and she agreed. Her father is not required to understand, or even accept, but his religion teaches tolerance and love. Her brother had not done something "evil," after all, just "odd." Therefore, one would expect her father to at least be polite and kind.

I suggested that Monique invite them both and let her father know that she loves him, appreciates how difficult it must be to deal with a son who surgically changed sex to a woman, appreciates his loss and pain, but that his rage and rejection changes nothing . . . except his heart.

"And then, Monique, let it be. And know that you are upholding important spiritual principles."

Although she was afraid her father might dump her too, she decided to stand by her principles. That is character.

Character doesn't look to zero in on goodies, it looks to do what's right and not find excuses to do what's wrong.

BUT . . . I DON'T SEE THE PROBLEM

Character may look to do what's right, but what happens when you just want to make nice-nice and make someone feel better right now because looking good is your basic goal.

I've had students-in-training over the years, and this was a recurrent issue. Some of the counseling students wanted to avoid confrontation, bad feelings, uncomfortable moments, and the possibility of not being "liked." Their behavior was then to serve their own needs, not the client's, and not the morality or reality of the situation. Consequently, they didn't want to *look* at what they needed to see, and have the client know.

I received this fax, which gives a great example:

> Dr. Laura, I was flipping through the radio dial and came across a talk show that was along the lines of yours in subject, but drastically different in substance. I heard a caller who was upset because his girlfriend's parents didn't accept him. When asked what he thought the problem was he said, "Well, I'm thirteen years older, she's twenty-one and I'm thirty-four, I'm black and she's white, I'm a recovering drug addict . . ." and then as an aside, "She's pregnant."
>
> The on-air therapist-host's response?
> "Are you in recovery for addiction?"
> "Yes."
> "Good for you! Now it's time to take the next step and marry her."
> And that was it!
> Dr. Laura, if you have the time, could you please call up this show and give them some advice? Seriously, though, I was infuriated. I had to write if only to vent. I listened more, and these two "hosts," under the guise of being qualified psychotherapists, continued to coddle all the callers, to ignore the real issues, and only try to make them feel good, without

ever pointing out any truth that might be "uncomfortable." AAGGH!
> Greg

Sometimes we do "wrong" simply because it is too taxing,
challenging, threatening, or uncomfortable to "bother" to do
"right." And, that is just plain wrong.

BUT . . . I GET OUTTA TROUBLE

Continuing along the line of protecting your butt: there are
folks who do wrong on top of wrong already done simply
because they are desperately trying to avoid consequences to
the first wrong! They don't see that they're just doubling the
risk of getting caught.

Karen, twenty-three, was on the verge of becoming one of
that sort—although she came on the air with me announcing
that she had a "little bit of a dilemma." As her story unfolded, I
came to see that no matter what she was bad at, Karen certainly excelled at understatement.

Seems her husband, whom she claimed to love to death,
was out of town on a ten-day business trip, and poor Karen
was feeling lonely. When a male acquaintance invited her
along for drinks with a group of his friends, she eagerly
accepted—and of course ended up having a heart-to-heart
with the guy. As the cocktail glasses piled up, the feelings
began spilling out. Her acquaintance was wrestling with his
own emotional problems and Karen's brother was dying, her
husband was away, and she needed some place for her pain to
go. Her pain and his body ended up in bed together.

Karen assured me she knew she'd made a mistake and had-
n't had any contact with her friend since the encounter. So how

did she get caught? Turns out she's pregnant—and her husband is infertile. Oops.

"Karen," I responded, "do you want professional advice or my personal opinion?"

"I guess your opinion."

"Well, if you're going to terminate the pregnancy there is no point in your telling anyone. I have a problem with your terminating the pregnancy. This is not an issue of violent rape, incest, or your physical safety. This is an issue of eliminating a small life to protect your reputation. There is an ironic side here. This conception took place because you wanted to sedate your pain over your brother's imminent death; the conclusion is yet another death?"

"There is no rational stuff about this," Karen countered, "it's all about emotion."

"But, Karen, we are rational and moral creatures. If the upcoming death of your brother is meaningful, then I don't understand how the death of your baby is not meaningful too. The baby's only fault is the situation of its conception—an oopsie. I realize that there is a more profound relationship with your brother than with this embryo. But morality implies values above and beyond emotion, don't you think?"

"I agree."

"My personal opinion and recommendation is that you tell your husband the truth. He has the option of the two of you raising the child as yours without ever telling the other guy"—as if it were artificial insemination by an anonymous donor—"or you put it up for adoption to a couple or the biological father if you think he wants to raise a child. If your husband is the man you love and trust, then this is something you deal with him about."

"I do. This is totally nothing like me at all."

"Honey, what you do is exactly 'like who' you are."

"I just don't want to hurt my husband."

"We both wish you'd felt that way that night!"

In addition to getting caught, Karen was waving the old "my action is nothing like me" excuse around like a banner. What she didn't get was that what you choose to do under difficult conditions speaks to who you are and what you are like, more than what you do in so-called normal times.

Our behaviors tell us who we are, not our fantasies about our ideal selves under ideal circumstances. Karen needed to accept that and challenge herself to have greater conscience and courage next time. Dealing with the husband about the pregnancy was actually giving her that second chance to measure who she is.

BUT . . . I GET GOODIES

That fatal night when she slept with her friend, Karen wanted some goodies. Now she doesn't want any baddies to come from it. Some people are so into goodies that they literally throw away any notions of bad or wrong. Take a caller named Jean, fifty-four.

She started by saying, "I'm facing something that I'd just rather bury my head in the sand about . . . "

"Yeah, Jean, but remember which end is sticking up in the air when you do that!"

Jean, a part-time travel writer, was on a trip to the Virgin Islands where she had unprotected sex with another travel writer whom she describes as the "worst and most selfish man I've ever slept with." So, what's the problem? He's invited her on a Caribbean cruise, and she's finding it hard to say no. Not only does the man have more professional connections than she does, she also wants the free trip—but just not sleep with him. But alas, that is part of the bargain.

"Do you know how outraged women get when they think men have wined and dined and flattered them only for sex?" I demanded. "It is immoral to use somebody. If you call him up and tell him you don't really like him and he is a lousy lover but you'll take this trip for the freebie aspects and the contacts—if he still wants to go, you have my warped blessing."

Jean's story is a good example of amorality—of simply not applying any notions of good and bad whatsoever to a situation in which acquisitivness is supreme.

From the Babylonian Talmud, Shabbat 31a, comes a story about a certain fellow who wished to be converted to Judaism and sought to learn the entire Torah while standing on one foot. The first rabbi so challenged chased him away with a stick. When he came before the great Rabbi Hillel, the wise man converted him and said, "What is hateful to you, do not do to your neighbor: this is the whole Torah. The rest is commentary; now go and study."

The moral of this story is that ethics in actions are everything to being a human being, a good human being.

BUT . . . IT WORKS FOR RIGHT NOW

Then there are the people who mistakenly behave as if a reprehensible action will have absolutely no relevance to, or impact on, their future.

Rick, twenty-five, was one of them. He was struggling with the idea of posing nude in the porn business to make a quick buck and used every rationalization in the book—from "uptight society," through "bodies are beautiful," to "freedom to do what I want"—as justification. I pointed out that his "beautiful body" would be exploited for prurient purposes and how unwise "freedom of action" now could haunt him in the future, and that "uptight" to one is sacred to another. Rick needed to understand that his present behaviors would be used to measure his integrity in times to come, whether or not he thought they should be. Generally he'd be seen as the kind of guy who, when the going got tough, would cut corners and get into slime.

Friends of my caller Elaine are startling examples of not seeing the future in the present:

> I have a thirty-seven-year-old friend who just had a baby with a confirmed jerk last week because she felt her biological clock was running out. It's only been a week since the birth and she wants out.
>
> I have another friend, twenty-five, with two girls, two and seven, never married, same father, has been on welfare, now works full time. She tells me that she's met the man of her dreams and wants to elope, after knowing him only two months. Never mind that he also has two kids in his custody and two more somewhere else, and is just now moving out of a live-in situation with another woman with kids. My friend's kids already call him Daddy, and she thinks it is destiny. I have begged her to wait at least a year . . . but no way. They have had unprotected sex one time already and she said that she doesn't want to 'live in sin' so that is another reason to hurry and get married. I said, 'Then don't have sex.' She said, 'I don't understand, it's impossible.' I told her to get Krazy Glue and put it between her knees.

I've made lotsa mistakes in my own life, and even though I try my best today I don't love my life all the time, and sometimes quietly resent it and hate myself for stupid, stupid decisions and ponder on how I screwed up our lives this far ... but the moment passes. I pick myself up, take care of my responsibilities, act with honor and integrity, make all my decisions with my kids' needs first because it is the right thing to do.

While I don't truly believe that all of tomorrow is indelibly inscribed by what you do today, it is true that each choice you make has consequences that either increase or decrease future options and opportunities. One trick I use with callers is to ask them to project themselves into what they'd like their future to be and then to ask themselves if this decision will help lead them there. Sometimes they recognize that they're being challenged to act with exceptional courage and conscience, and sometimes it seems like they just don't care.

BUT . . . FRANKLY, MY DEAR, I DON'T REALLY GIVE A DAMN

Speaking of folks who can't/won't see beyond their own immediate, selfish needs and wants, here's a story you'll find as unbelievable as I did—with a postscript that will amaze you. When Stan, forty-one, called about his ex-wife and his six-year-old son, I was initially dubious about what he was saying because custody skirmishes bring out the worst in terms of distortions and outright lies.

Stan's ex is with a new fellow whose thirteen-year-old boy molested Stan's six-year-old son. The ex still sees her boy every other weekend. However, by court order, the thirteen-year-old is removed from the house for the duration of the visit. Now comes the kicker. Stan's ex wants him to switch visitation weekends so the six-year-old can attend her wedding to the molester's father—at which the thirteen-year-old will also be, in violation of the court order.

When Stan asked for my advice, I strongly suggested he protect his son by refusing to switch the dates as long as the thirteen-year-old was to be present at the ceremony. He thanked me, assured me he was going to take my advice, and I hung up thinking that was the end of it.

Wrong!!!!

Later that afternoon, I was in my office when the ex called. Although she'd heard my conversation with Stan, she didn't recognize my voice and presumed I was an assistant. I didn't set her straight. At first she claimed that Dr. Laura hadn't gotten all the pertinent information before making her recommendation, but when I asked her if the molestation and court order were correct, she said yes. "Then," I asked, "what didn't Dr. Laura get right?" "Well," she said with annoyance, "there must be some other way to protect my son besides not coming to the party!"

Frankly, I almost dropped my teeth, but managed to calmly inquire, "How about leaving the thirteen-year-old out of it?" "Oh," she replied ever so sweetly, "I couldn't do that. It would hurt his feelings." "Well," I tried again, "perhaps you could marry into a family without child molesters."

Since I was off the air and not playing myself, I gave myself some leeway for that bit of sarcasm, then went on to tell her I was stunned at her seeming lack of concern over her little boy's feelings and welfare. She was still cursing me out when I quietly hung up the receiver.

I felt I had just conversed with evil. Evil human beings are more commonplace than you would imagine, and more dangerous than you would like to believe. They are usually recognized when they cold-bloodedly murder, as in a drive-by shooting or a robbery. They are less usually recognized, yet suffered all the same, as they work to diminish, punish, humiliate, abuse, and finally destroy the spirit of another.

There is a world of difference in doing wrong (as clarified in this chapter) and doing evil. Those who do wrong, as we've seen in the vignettes, actually know and care about the wrongdoing, even if they clearly drag their feet in doing anything about it. Generally, those who do wrong use all sorts of behaviors and psychological tricks to avoid truths that make them feel uncomfortable. But they call me because, on some level, they acknowledge the wrongness; ultimately, they are willing to look at themselves with critical (read painful) objectivity; i.e., they admit to appropriate guilt.

Evil has no such desire for self-examination, change, or growth. In fact, those are all seen as threats to the determined idealized version of the self. To maintain that inner and external guise evil types will literally do anything, without motivation to be good or do right. Evil is never self-critical, only other-critical, and does not have or admit to any guilt.

I remember a PBS special in the 1980s on the Los Angeles Hillside Strangler wherein a female psychiatrist was being interviewed on her professional assessment of someone who would perpetrate such heinous crimes. The doctor seemed nervous and uncomfortable with the question, hesitatingly offering that sometimes there was no psychiatric diagnosis, sometimes there was just evil.

It was the ex's frantic concern for having revelers at her wedding party, without any (I mean *any*) interest shown to the impact on her son from the continued exposure to a predator, that was the stunning invitation to evil. She really didn't care about her son at all. In her hands, he could eventually be destroyed.

Stan showed courage in the face of a blatant wrong, which is impressive since, I think, most folks are frightened of and intimidated by people who are right in their face doing something wrong. You know that's true. When you're trying to do something sneakily, you know to behave as though you're supposed to be there doin' that, right? The more confidence you project, the less others feel confidence to confront. Their callous confidence even makes you question yourself.

WHAT TO DO WHEN "WRONG" INVITES YOU IN

The next example shows Aaron in that black hole. Aaron, twenty-two, didn't waste any time beating around the bush with me: "My girlfriend wants my baby."

"You have a baby and she wants it?"

"No, she wants to make one with me. And I'm not ready. She said she's twenty-eight now and doesn't want to be thirty without a baby."

"Clearly, she's not, Aaron."

"She says that she doesn't mind that the father is not with her."

"She doesn't mind? Do you think the baby might mind not having a daddy? If you were the child you wouldn't want a father around?"

"Of course I would."

"Then you cannot be irresponsible and produce a baby without a family just to humor her. That she could just go out and make a baby and not care about the baby's best interest first shows that she is not ready to be a mother. She's selfish, self-centered, and immature, and you ought to tell her off."

"She seems so sure that this is okay."

"Maybe so. But you know something different. You know that the best bet for a child is an intact, two-parent home. What kind of woman would forsake that truth for what she wants to do just to do it?"

"Apparently not a woman ready for a family."

"Thank you, Aaron, now you go tell her that!"

Aaron is at one of those big turning points in life when someone is obviously doing something that's wrong but you're afraid to tell him or her it's wrong when you know you should. And that is just as wrong! Sadly, it's likely that when Aaron gives his girlfriend his opinion, he'll be dumped for another sperm donor. But at least he'd have done the right thing.

This not judging others really gets me going. If, indeed, there shalt be no judging, then where do we get laws and basic rules of conduct upon which we can all be free and upon which we can count on each other?

Greg Louganis, the Olympic diving champion, admitted to not having told the physician who sewed up his bleeding scalp at the 1988 games that he was HIV-positive—thus not taking into account that he might possibly be threatening the life of the man who was using his expertise to help him. I'm cognizant of all the arguments about scaring other athletes and setting the games into a tizzy. However, none of these lines of defense negates responsibility to another individual. I was impressed when many high-profile homosexual and lesbian individuals echoed my sentiments.

Still, there are those who can't shake the no-judgment mode. A good example is a letter to the editor in the *Los Angeles Daily News* that ended with, "Until you have walked not a mile—but those exact minutes—in Louganis' shoes, do not even presume to judge him."

I think that is a stupid comment. No one can ever walk in someone's shoes, life, or mind for any time at all and morality transcends individual circumstance and weaknesses. I think it's fair to explain why you did wrong—as long as it remains clear that a wrong has been done. And it takes courage to do right under circumstances of potential loss. Mr. Louganis didn't have it.

I seem to remember a nutrition book entitled something like *You Are What You Eat*. (Maybe I should retitle this chapter "You Are What You *Do*.") Face it, it is bad to do wrong, especially when you persist in the knowledge of its wrongness. Doing wrong, having regrets and remorse followed by redress, is the behavior of a basically good person. Consistently doing wrongs, compounding wrongs with more of the same, scapegoating while denying contribution to the wrongness eventually makes you a bad person. This statement of mine was challenged by someone who recently interviewed me. "How can you ever say someone is bad? Isn't it just the deed that was bad?"

How do you know a person if not by the consistent nature of the person's deeds? So, measure yours because we'll be measuring you.

3

✧

I Know It's Right . . .
But . . .

(Where's Your Courage?)

Always do right. This will gratify some people,
and astonish the rest.

Mark Twain

Most of the time when people call me with a decision to
make, they ask, "I don't know what the best thing to do is."
Rarely will someone say, "I don't know what the *right* thing to
do is." I think that is very telling. Perhaps it's imagined that if
you inquire about the "best" solution rather than the "right"
solution, your personal concerns will more likely be given due
consideration. The "right way" promises sacrifice and nobility.
Those are rarely self-serving enough to be of immediate gratification or comfort. The "best way," on the other hand, dangles
the prospect of some compromise of principles to give room
for immediate gratification or comfort.

BUT . . . I'D RATHER BE A VICTIM

Pete's whole life was about comfort. The irony was how uncomfortable that perpetual search truly made him. Pete, thirty-one, is married to a woman, forty, who abuses alcohol and cocaine and other assorted drugs. She went into a rehab program some six years ago, has since relapsed, and refuses to bother with it again because she doesn't like the burdens and restrictions put on her.

"I have a hard time dealing with this," Pete complained. "I believe in my marital vows, but do you stay married to someone like this? I've been known to play the martyr before. But, is it marriage at all costs?"

"No, Pete, I don't believe that," I responded. "Each of us has the moral obligation to bring forth our best self or at least work toward that with the support of the spouse. However, when one of us refuses to do either, then there is only half a marriage. I am a huge believer in commitment and vows, but it needs to be mutual. If you were beating her I'd tell her to leave. In a way, she's beating you."

"She says she is powerless over these things," Pete moaned.

"Well, my man, the whole time she was clean and sober she wasn't powerless, was she?"

"No, I guess not. That's right, actually."

"Pete, what is your biggest worry? Your vows or that if you leave you'd be a martyr without a cause?"

Pete laughed. "Yeah, I do play the victim."

"You play victim because . . . ?"

Pete came out with a list of five reasons he plays the victim. Here's the list. Sound familiar?

1. Because it gives me attention and something to focus on.

2. Because I don't want to have to feel guilty taking such a step as leaving a marriage or relationship or situation.
3. I'm lazy about accomplishments on my own.
4. I don't want to be responsible for choices in my life.
5. I hide, become invisible, hide behind someone else's identity.

"Well, Pete, those are powerful reasons to stay in this 'sick' situation, or find a new sick situation."

"I agree, I see that."

"Both of you are similar, do you see that, Pete? Both of you have trouble facing self and world. She uses drugs, you use suffering over your plight with her. So just leaving her is insufficient."

"Right, it's changing myself."

"Yes, that's right. So, instead of wondering if you are a bad person if you leave this confirmed druggie, I think you need for focus in on, 'I'm too scared to leave a druggie because then I have nothing to complain about, and if I have nothing to complain about I am lost.' "

It is right to stand by your partner. It is also right to protect yourself from the ongoing destructiveness of self-destructive people, no matter what relationship they have to you, including being "your woman." When those two "rights" collide, then other personal issues, like Pete's fear of autonomy, shift the balance of decision-making.

Pete was struggling with two issues: the guilt of walking away from a seriously troubled person to whom you've made a commitment and the fear of facing a life without someone else to hold accountable for your pain and failure. This is a sticky mess, and Pete was stuck in it.

Let me put the abandonment-in-times-of-pain issue in perspective. Yes, it is right to be giving. But, it is foolish to be giving when what you give is constantly abused, disrespected, unappreciated, and not reciprocated. Yes, it is right to be loyal. It is foolish to be loyal when it supports illegal or immoral activities or when, after significant and sincere due time and effort, the other person consistently refuses to cooperate in his or her own welfare. When such foolishness is rationalized as right behavior, be aware it is most usually a way to hide from reality, from life, from your courageous self.

BUT . . . I DID THE RIGHT THING AND I'M STILL MISERABLE

When the right or healthy thing to do might be to leave, there might be an immediate high of relief getting away from the madness—or an immediate low from the fear of being alone with a whole bunch of challenging realities about yourself, others, or the situation. In leaving and being alone with yourself, you may discover a frightening truth: you didn't stay with the drug user/alcohol abuser/abuser/philanderer out of love or compassion. You stayed because those challenging realities seemed more difficult and painful to confront than the suffering over the user/abuser. Imagine that.

A listener's letter confirms this truth:

> Hi, Dr. Laura!
>   You gave me some advice about two and a half years ago concerning my abusive relationship with my ex. You told me to leave, I have, and have been legally divorced for one and a half years. I'm working and supporting myself and two kids. But, I'm finding myself increasingly depressed and tired. If I did the right thing, why is my life not going great,

and why am I not happy all of the time?

I would love to do things. However, I don't have the dollars to do so, and I'm so tired all the time. What's up with this?

I'm embarrassed to say so, but at times, man, this life is HELL! At least I did not have to do it all when I was with him. Everyone says things will get better and I'll find someone special. I'm not so sure.

Love, Elizabeth

There are two important aspects of Elizabeth's letter: first, "Why is my life not going great, and why am I not happy all of the time?" and second, "I'll find someone special."

The first aspect indicates an immature view of life. For no one is life perpetually great. In any case, research indicates that it is not the greatness of how life is going that makes an individual happy, it is attitude. I am reminded here of some lines from the Nobel Prize-winning Indian poet Rabinranath Tagore:

I slept and dreamt that life was Joy.
I woke and saw that life was Duty.
I acted, and behold, Duty was Joy.

The quality of our lives is not created solely by the events in our lives. It is in our unique response to life that we define our lives. Michael Harris wrote in the *Los Angeles Times:* "Human problems, are simply that: problems. Problems are life, not just occasions for therapy. If things happen to get better, that's life too."

Elizabeth now laments leaving battering for difficult burdens. She is wondering what the gain was. Well, for one thing, she's not being battered and her children are no longer being emotionally or physically scarred. Now she has the opportunity to build her life a new way. One of the reasons she got involved with, in her words, "a powerful, controlling" fellow in the first place was her lack of willingness to be her own engine. Now, belatedly, she has that opportunity, but she's still looking for magic.

The second aspect, "find someone special" could be a deadly trap at this point if Elizabeth doesn't come to admire the possibilities of her own autonomy instead of imagining that a relationship will be salvation from life's challenges.

BUT . . . IT'S SO NEW AND I'M SO SCARED

The future is the unknown. The past, no matter how lousy it was, is familiar. Unknown *vs.* Familiar. Which usually wins out?

Most folks tend to cling to the familiar. Carla's call gave clear evidence of that:

"I need to ask you a simple question and make sure I'm going to be doing the right thing," Carla, thirty, groaned into the telephone.

"Wait a minute, Carla, do you believe whatever it is would be the right thing?"

"Yes, I do, but . . . "

"Carla, if you drop the 'but' and just sit with the statement that you are doing the right thing, what does that feel like?"

"The fear of the unknown and the change."

"You know you're doing the right thing, but you're uncomfortable with unknown and change—you're scared. What is so bad about being scared?"

"It is a risk you have to take in life. It is part of life."

"Yes! You go on the freeway, you take a risk. You get a haircut, you take a risk."

"Thank you, Laura. I just wanted to know I made the right choice."

"Carla, I don't even know what you're choosing between—we never got to the specifics. I didn't tell you that you made the right choice. You already knew that. The point is that you've probably made the 'right' decision, you're just very scared. But you can handle scared, you've been there and done that—you just don't remember. Give me an example of how you handled 'scared' to do some other 'right' thing."

"Ummm, I ran a marathon. I was scared of getting hurt, quitting and looking like an idiot. But I was willing to pay whatever price to experience doing it. And it was worth it."

"And, won't this situation be worth it also?"

"Yes, it would."

"Then do it!"

BUT . . . I'M NOT REALLY SELLING OUT, AM I?

There is a law of physics that states that for every action there is an equal and opposite reaction. The same principle applies to human action. That's where courage comes in, because doing the right thing carries its own price tag. Where ethics are concerned, there is rarely a free lunch.

Linda said she needed some advice about coping in the workplace.

"What does 'coping' mean to you?" I asked in order to find out what she really wanted.

She hesitated and then offered that it was "How to get through the day and still keep a positive attitude."

"You mean," I continued to probe, "how not to let something unpleasant or inappropriate bother you?"

"Right."

"Linda, you're willing to accept it—whatever it is—is not going to change, you're not going to try to change it, nor will you leave it. You simply want to get through it with a smile."

"Yeah," she responded, "I don't want it to affect my positive outlook. This situation is the vehicle to get me to where I want to go."

"So you want to hang in but lay low with something bad because you've got bigger plans. You need to tolerate things you don't really accept because of bigger rewards down the pike. Let me ask you something without knowing what the specific problem in question is. Are you selling out?"

"Am I selling out?" she replied incredulously.

"Yeah, because you want something down the line are you tolerating something you ought not tolerate?"

"Ummm, am I selling out? Yes, I guess I am," she offered sadly.

"You want me to help you sell out? How long have you been listening to me?" (Linda and I both laughed.)

"Oh, you got me good, Dr. Laura! So let me change my question. I've opened my mouth and started getting negative feedback that put some pressure on me."

"I understand that, and I understand that you want your pot of gold at the end of the rainbow, but you'll have to stand by and watch something wrong continue to do that. That is selling out."

"Oh, I didn't think of it as being bad. Well, how do I do this?"

"You don't sell out."

"I open my mouth and say something?"

"Well, I don't know how joyous that pot o' gold will be when you look back on how you got it. I don't think you can cope with something you find unethical or immoral. So, the answer is . . . "

"Don't sell out."

"Linda, I know you'll handle it with honor."

Well, Linda did handle this situation with honor—and it cost her big time. I know because she wrote me a month after we talked. This issue, by the way, was her observations of racial discrimination of co-workers in a major department store.

Linda put herself on the line for her co-workers, for a principle. And this is what happened to her:

After speaking to you, I went back into work and spoke with my supervisor. I told her I would not "sell out" and look the other way when inappropriate behavior or injustices were displayed by her and the other executives. I also told her that I felt I had an obligation as a supervisor to set an example for my crew. I also went in and spoke with my personnel manager. During our conversation, I told him "I am not going to sell out.'"

The next day, when I arrived at work, I was asked to report to the store manager's office. I was given a Phase I warning notice as the first step in disciplinary action. My supervisor justified this action with examples of hearsay and refused to tell me who my accusers were.

However, I am not writing you to say, "poor me." I am writing to say, "thank you." You helped me to realize I would not feel wonderful if I looked the other way. I would not earn respect from my co-workers and crew if I jumped on the executive's abuse band wagon. I now realize I have a more active conscience than I gave myself credit for. And now I know, I would not and could not sell out at any job just to have a paycheck.

I must admit, I was angry, hurt, and scared. I am a person who HAD breast cancer (tomorrow is my five-year survival anniversary). I needed this job to have medical benefits and to work around my school schedule. What I didn't need from this job was the abuse and power-trip displayed by four of the six executives at my store.

So, again, I want to thank you for NOT teaching me: How To Sell Out.

Linda's story is a perfect illustration of one of those special, personal moments when you must choose between an act of convenience and an act of conviction. It is this choice that defines your happiness. It is this choice that defines your character.

Choosing conscience in the face of fear was the kind of decision Jeanne was wrestling with when she wrote, "And I am afraid that if I do what is right for my grandchildren, I will lose my daughter forever." She'd described at length the maternal unfitness of her perpetually drug-abusing daughter (the children were born with drugs in their bloodstream) who found one abusive guy after another and put her major efforts into unlawful activities.

My husband and myself have decided to legally take my daughter's two children away from her because we feel she is an unfit mother. But since that decision I have had a great many second thoughts . . . or, I guess the real fact is that I have loads of fears.

I am afraid that my daughter will never be able

to forgive me. It scares me to think that the young woman that I was so close to for so many years can lie and cheat and not give it a second thought.

I didn't believe for a moment that Jeanne was truly having second thoughts. Deep in her heart, she knew that not taking serious action wouldn't change her daughter or protect the children. Jeanne is anguishing over the painful reality that her daughter is a total loss.

If Jeanne acts, if Jeanne does the right thing by her grand-children, it will be the final nail in the coffin of her giving up on her daughter—of her fantasies about "perfect mothering" and "perfect families" being all-powerful as deterrents of evil. Well, it just ain't so. All people pick their way through life. Some folks just pick a bad way.

After I read Jeanne's letter on the air and gave my assess-ment, I received a fax from a woman who urged Jeanne to take the kids:

I am listening to you as I type this . . . your advice to the grandmother is so right. Take the kids! Screw your daughter! I went through the exact same thing with my sister . . . the kids are the most impor-tant issue here. If drugs are more important to these people, then there is nothing you can do. The one thing you can do, the only right thing to do, is to save the children. Period.

By the way, two years later my sister did forgive me. But now, she has done it again. New child, no husband, and back on drugs. Tell that woman to keep the kids until they are out of high school and head-ing toward college or as long as she can. Some peo-ple never learn. My sister hasn't.

RIGHT SHOULDN'T NEED
WRONG'S FORGIVENESS

You know, I'm genuinely fascinated by good people who worry about the forgiveness of wrongdoers. Seems like it should be the other way around, don't you think?

Good people, people who act out of conscience and courage, seem to have a tough time understanding the blatantly bad actions of others because they can't really comprehend the desire to do wrong, the thrill of doing wrong, and the lack of conscience to control that impulse. Therefore, they struggle to find excuses to explain away the bad behaviors as actions over which the perpetrators had no control. A history of abuse has become the vogue excuse for begging exoneration for acts ranging from naughty, to wrong, to downright evil.

Dr. Bruno Bettelheim, imprisoned at both Buchenwald and Dachau, concluded from his experiences that a concentration camp inmate's personality dissolution began with the moment he or see started justifying wrong behavior as caused by outside oppression. "Blaming others," he wrote in *The Informed Heart*, "or outside conditions for one's own misbehavior may be the child's privilege; if an adult denies responsibility for his own actions, it is another step toward personality disintegration."

There are hardly many everyday parallels between the terror, cruelty, and inhumanity of a concentration camp and the disappointments, frustrations, and challenges of most lives. And even under such horrible duress, we each retain the freedom to exercise our humanity in choosing our actions.

Dr. Viktor Frankl in *Man's Search for Meaning* elaborated on this idea: "We who lived in concentration camps can remember the men who walked through the huts comforting others, giving away their last piece of bread. They may have been few in number, but they offer sufficient proof that everything can be taken away from a man but one thing: the last of the human freedoms—to choose one's attitude in any given set of circumstances, to choose one's own way."

Abuse! Victim! Garbage! People generally choose their bad company. People choose routes that are easier even if they're destructive. People choose their actions and reactions. And they should be held accountable for these choices and the consequences of those actions, no matter what the history or the present circumstances. When we move away from that imperative, we move away from being human and move closer to being animal.

BUT . . . IT'S WHERE ANGELS FEAR TO TREAD

Adrianna, twenty, is having a devil of a time doing right in the face of badness. She lives in the same apartment complex as her twenty-three-year-old sister, whose live-in boyfriend has his six-year-old son visiting for the summer. Claiming they'll only be away for an hour, they were dumping the kid on her and taking off—sometimes for days. Adrianna is uncomfortable saying anything "too strong" to her sister, even though she is thoroughly shocked and disgusted by the total lack of regard both her sister and her boyfriend have for this little boy. She acknowledges their self-centeredness, immaturity, and cruelty, but is so intimidated by the boldness of their demeanors and behaviors that she is overwhelmed to the point of helplessness.

Good point. When people are so blatantly bad it is so difficult for good folks to cope. Fearful of having that badness directed at them, they feel powerless confronting it. Think about it. When someone gets real bad in your face, do you really believe simply bringing the error of their ways to their attention will have any impact? No way! So, you do nothing.

I suggested she tell her sister and the boyfriend they're doing the wrong thing and that if they don't start behaving responsibly, she'll personally call and let the boy's mother know about it. I ended up by warning Adrianna that she'd just have to tolerate the discomfort of confrontation because the boy was depending on her to be strong—someone had to protect him.

WHEN DOING RIGHT DOESN'T GET UNIVERSAL APPLAUSE

Good people have another problem when dealing with bad people. Good people are, by definition, very committed to the rules. It seems difficult for good people to break the rules even to stop a greater wrong. That was definitely a problem for Sharla.

Sharla's sister is single, has a one-and-a-half-year-old son, and is doing drugs. The problem was that she confided the drug use to Sharla and swore her to secrecy. Sharla's rule is not to betray a confidence, so she tried to talk her sister into rehab. When that didn't work, she broke her rule and blew the whistle to Child Protective Service. Her sister managed to pull one off, and CPS didn't file. Now the sister is furious at Sharla's betrayal of confidence, and the family is all upset about the so-called scandal—even more than the drug use!

"I'm carrying around guilt that I destroyed my family. Everyone is against me," Sharla literally cried. I told Sharla she'd done the right thing, and that cannot be measured by the inappropriate reactions of others. Now that's a tough one, because we all imagine that doing the right thing will get us a ticker tape parade or at least admiring eyes.

"Sharla," I asked her, "do you feel in your heart you did the right thing?"

"Yes," she replied without hesitating. "But it's just so painful to be hated for it."

"You did the right thing and you are the only one in your family with a clear conscience," I reminded her.

"Yeah, I guess that's true really, it's just that it doesn't show."

"But ultimately, that's what shows you to be a good person, a person of character. Remember these wise, ancient words, 'Even if you are a minority of one, the truth is the truth.'"

In point of fact, Sharla was being punished for doing the right thing because others didn't want to deal with the wrongdoing. If they dealt with it they'd have to face issues of guilt for either helping to cause the problems or not acting to solve the problems. In these circumstances, doing good may not show to the world, but it gives you the personal satisfaction of knowing you did right—that you are a person of courage.

BUT . . . IF I SEE NO EVIL . . .

Turning your back on a problem or on something wrong doesn't make it go away or turn it right. On the contrary, ignoring bad behaviors usually contributes to making things worse. I wonder if some basically good people don't have a deep-down worry that if they deal with bad, they'll have to confront some bad that does reside, or did reside, inside themselves. Maybe "seeing no evil" outside is a way to avoid the recognition of potential evil internally. That's the dilemma my caller Margaret, fifty, was grappling with.

She was justifiably upset because in the course of cleaning her fourteen-year-old son's room she found a long letter from a thirty-seven-year-old man, which, in her words, "was long and rambling and made my skin crawl. It was like he was coming on to my son. I don't know how to face this," she said unhappily.

"I think you know what to do, Margaret. I wonder if you are uncomfortable doing it because it comes with some large price tag," I guessed. I asked her what that price tag might be, and she grudgingly replied, "Well, it would mean communication with my son."

"And that hasn't been too good up to now, right?"

"Well, I was snooping."

"Parents don't require a search warrant, just sufficient cause, Margaret. Would you rather just let this go than struggle with communication and admit to snooping?"

"No."

"So, Margaret, to deal with this situation, we have to deal with the fact that the letter writer and your son are both male, with the homosexual implication rattling your teeth, right?"

"Oh, ohhh," she gasped, "I never even thought of that."

"Margaret, your denial is astonishing!"

"Well, I thought maybe it was one-sided."

"Part of the price tag, then, would be to find out it's two-sided, that your son might be homosexual. So basically this is not 'I don't know what to do,' this is 'I don't want to find out something which will upset me.'

"Margaret," I insisted, "the fact of whether or not you get upset is secondary to the welfare of your child. Now, taking your feelings out of the picture, what do you think you should do?"

"Call this older man and tell him this behavior is inappropriate and it must stop."

"Or . . . ?"

"Or . . . I don't have any power, do I?"

"Report him to authorities. Margaret, are you a married lady? Is there a dad at home? Sometimes young boys fall prey to such men because they are bereft of that attachment at home."

"Well," she admitted, "that's possibly the case. My husband, his dad, lives in our home, but he's not real strong. He doesn't interact with his son a lot . . . I guess."

"You guess? This boy is living in a home with shadows of parents?"

"Yeah, you're right," she told me. "I have to stop living in shadows and take solid form and act. Thank you."

Margaret did not want to deal with her sad marriage, her lack of communication with her son, his potential homosexuality, or his desperate need for interaction from strong, involved parental types. Taking on all these issues meant examining her own limitations, mistakes, fears, etc. In the end, I was glad Margaret found the letter because it could provide the springboard to pulling this family together in a healthier way.

Not wanting to face something external lest it alert you to something wrong inside the past (i.e., not wanting to judge or confront someone else's inappropriate behaviors because of your lingering guilt about having once done the same thing) or present (not wanting to find out you may have contributed to the problem through your faults and weaknesses) is a powerful motivation for not doing right. Unfortunately, not doing right does not leave you with a void. It leaves you with a wrong.

BUT . . . IT'S NOT WHAT I PLANNED

Michael, twenty, was facing doing right after being wronged. For about ten months, he'd been having a sexual relationship with a young woman who'd been on birth control pills. He'd made his feelings about not wanting to have children perfectly clear to her. Nonetheless, she intentionally went off the pill seven months earlier without telling him. And now—surprise—she's pregnant.

"Since then we've broken up and I feel very responsible for the kid, but I don't want her in my life in any way. And I feel like she did it to keep me in her life. She told some friends that she knew of situations like this where the father eventually came around and they lived happily ever after. I can't see that happening. I feel responsible for the kid, but I don't know what to do because I'm so angry with her."

"Michael, your ego is in the way. She got you by the short hairs and you're angry."

"Yeah," he enthusiastically agreed, "this is emotional blackmail."

"Michael, one sentence should clear this all up for you. Here it is: the child doesn't care about all these shenanigans. It just wants a daddy."

"Will the feeling I have toward her rub off on the kid?"

"Only if you stay in hurt ego mode and behave like a jerk. The reality is that you had intercourse in an unmarried situation—you took a risk! Even if she used the pill all the time, you took a risk because some women, though it's rare, do get pregnant on the pill. If you didn't want to have kids you could have used a condom or gotten a vasectomy. You could have taken control of your life. You didn't. That created life. You got yourself into this problem, not your lady. Ultimately, you took the risk, now you have to be father."

"Dr. Laura, I guess you kinda like told me what I was leaning toward anyway. Is there a way I can see my kid and never have her in my life?"

"No," I answered. "For the sake of the kid you've got to learn to get along and be nice to each other. It seems to me you ought to be able to sit in a room and look at her if you were able to get naked and do it with her. There are people in your life you don't like and you find a way to be polite. Now, Michael, sit with her and explain that there will not be a love relationship between you two, but that you intend to parent this child. Other things: see an attorney together and work out the legalities of living arrangements and visitation."

"Also, Michael," I concluded, "realize that you are stuck with each other for two decades. When either one of you marries you'll have to live close to each other for the ability to parent this child. This is one good reason not to have intercourse with someone you don't want to be connected to for life! You have created a twenty-year destiny through some orgasms. Hope they were worth it."

BUT . . . IT'S NOT CONVENIENT

Michael and his lady and their eventual spouses are going to be mighty inconvenienced by the tangled web they wove when first they practiced to conceive! Nonetheless, at least they were both facing up to some portion of the current reality: a baby, a new human being.

Granted, the circumstances and timing were lousy, especially for the welfare of this child, but perfect timing, perfect conditions never happen. What makes human beings special is that we have the courage and conscience to rise to the occasion and do what is difficult when we know it is right.

Jean, forty, happily married twenty years with two children, ten and seventeen, has just discovered that she is pregnant—by accident (actually, by intercourse, but I'll leave that nag for later).

She and her husband have a lot of doubts about continuing the pregnancy, including her age and the drain on their finances. Jean appreciated that she was wrestling with a moral dilemma whose consequences she would have to live with for the rest of her life. "How do you make such a decision?" she pleaded. "How do you live with the decision?"

"Well, Jean, only one of those decisions brings hugs and touching memories. That's one option to have to live with."

"Yes, and if I terminate, there will be guilt with me for the rest of my life. How do I cope with that?"

"Is your question how do you terminate without feeling bad?"

"Yes, I guess so."

"I would hope that when people do that they would feel bad. That is what feeling bad is supposed to be about. It is part of the human psyche and spirit, it is what makes us special that certain of our acts causes us so much emotional repercussion. That is what makes us special and termites not. Termites don't go into confession after they eat your house, you know."

"Laura, what do you hear from people about starting kids at this age?"

"I had my son when I was thirty-eight. First and only. I was an infertility patient and lucky to have that one!"

"It's ironic, Dr. Laura. I was an infertility patient for the second. And here I was seventeen years ago going through the same dilemma because our first wasn't planned. He's great. Both of them are. We make great kids."

"I guess, Jean, that plural 'kids' just got more pluralized. What the world needs now, is more 'great' kids."

"I feel that, it's just juggling everything . . . "

"I didn't say it would be easy, but you've got practice, right?"

"Right!"

"I just feel, Jean, that it is the 'right' thing."

"You do?" Jean sounded as if a great weight had been lifted from her shoulders. "I do too. In my heart of hearts I know that to be true."

SOMETIMES YOU HAVE TO GRIT YOUR TEETH TO DO RIGHT

My message to Jean was that decisions based on behaviors that don't necessarily make life easier are the ones that most ennoble us. Such actions may not serve our needs for immediate personal and interpersonal gratification, but they do serve our spiritual selves. Ironically, a focus on serving our spiritual selves does have ramifications of protection and elevation of our physical selves. Brent's letter may sound too good—but it's true:

> I am writing this letter to people my age who will probably not hear too many similar stories elsewhere. I am twenty-five and engaged to be married in June. I am an aspiring musician and teacher, my fiancée is a student who eventually will teach. We have been together through many difficult situations, and because of our long relationship, we have always thought of ourselves as responsible young adults. The reason I stress this fact is that during the last two years we have had a very active sex life. Quite frankly, we are two of the horniest little gits you could imagine!
>
> We've been careful; she is on the pill and I

always use condoms. Truth be told, we always joked between ourselves that if she were to get pregnant, we would have to name the kid Jesus. Nonetheless, we still waited eagerly for the end of each month to roll around and let us know that once again we were "home free."

I began listening to your program several weeks ago, and, true to your intentions, my conscience has been niggling me. Was our talking about the risks involved in sex enough? Was I really "making love" to my fiancée when the very act, while making us feel closer and more intimate, carried with it the risk of depriving her of the dreams and goals she had striven for so ambitiously?

After wrestling with my libido for several days, my conscience won out. The risk of an unwanted pregnancy was there, no matter how small. Don't misunderstand, we both want kids desperately, but we want to have them when it will be best for our children. That time is not when my fiancée is in the running for several prestigious graduate scholarship and I'm struggling to make it in a very competitive career.

I decided to tell my fiancée that I thought we should stop having sex.

To my surprise, she had been feeling much the same way. Nonetheless, even between two people as intimate as we are, it was not an easy topic to be frank about.

You find yourself looking at each other and saying things like, "We don't believe in abortion, but do we really want to have to make that choice?" Of course, as soon as you ask the question, the answer becomes clear; you don't have to make that decision.

With a little self-control it never becomes an issue, does it? As I said, not an easy topic to broach, but as you watch your rationalizations melt away, it's amazing how plainly the truly responsible decision presents itself to you.

It took a lot of teeth-gritting, frustrated exclamations, and hugs of encouragement, but we made it through the worst moments and kept our word. Every time since, when things get hot and sweaty, we find ourselves laughing together, exclaiming, "I can't wait until we're married!" knowing that our resolve is firm.

So, take heart, fellow Dr. Laura listeners! The youth of today are not the mindless minx that the Donahues and Joycelyn Elders of the world make us out to be! You don't have to have sex just because you've been doing it all along. Take it from us, it's going to be a long year, but the sacrifice of doing the right thing, particularly for the sake of other people (the as-yet unborn children you've never met), ennobles you and makes the wait worthwhile.

BUT . . . I JUST DON'T WANNA . . .

"Ennobles you." I am swept away by Brent's realization, at twenty-five, that behaviors do not just serve our physical and interpersonal needs, but that behaviors serve spiritual needs as well. So many people, like Laura, thirty-four, are stuck in the former.

Laura has been married for ten years. Her husband is a "wonderful guy" who worked to put her through law school. Now that's she's finished and working as an attorney, they're financially ecstatic. However, there's one rift in the ecstasy; he now wants her to reciprocate and support him while he goes to law school.

After listening to her give me all sorts of reasonable sounding complaints about the strain of being sole support and her nervousness over how their future depends on what kinds of grades he gets, I asked her to put that all aside and tell me the embarrassing part of all of this for her.

"I really don't like being broke again at thirty-five. I'm embarrassed by it. I really don't like to say to my friends, 'No, we can't go out to dinner with you, we don't have the money.' I did this at twenty, and as much as I want to support him I'm doing a lousy job at this and I'm disappointed with myself."

"You're being pouty because this all means sacrifice," I suggested.

"And I've been there and done that."

"You've been there and done that for yourself, Laura. Never before for anyone else."

"Whoa . . . oh . . . "

"Laura, this is an attitude issue. Yes, I know you can't do the things your more well-to-do friends can do, but that's because you're being a loving partner. You need to think of this situation as a loving choice, not lousy fate. Your success was about doin' and lookin' a certain way. Real-life success is about doing good and looking to the needs of others. This is a time of spiritual growth, where your generosity provides stronger glue for the relationship and strengthens your character. That's a lot to think about."

BUT . . . IT'S NOT FAIR

Being good and doing right certainly have their challenging stresses and strains, as we've seen so far in this chapter.

Tolerating someone else's goodness is sometimes a pain in the neck also—if you can believe that! That's why Brenda, fifty, was so disgusted.

"I'm calling you in reference to money," she began forthrightly. "My husband is a military soldier and he's been sending his elderly mother money for eighteen years. He has nine siblings who live in her area. He's being the most responsible. I just don't think its fair."

"Now, Brenda, let me get this clear. You're complaining because you married the one out of the ten children who is an ethical person. I can't believe you are complaining that you married a good guy."

She went on to defend her position by saying, "I guess I was mostly looking at the other siblings who are not doing right."

I countered with, "You certainly don't fault someone for being a good person just because everyone around them isn't."

"Oh, my gosh, that is right, isn't it."

Brenda was starting to look at the situation backward when she wondered why her husband should do right if no one else does. Not only was she bothered by the unfairness, but also by the ongoing sacrifice of money she and her husband were making because of others' lack of responsibility.

We didn't get to it, but perhaps the other siblings are contributing in different ways, for instance by contributing time and effort to help Mom. Nonetheless, this issue of determining whether right should be done in the shadow of "wrongs" is one many people struggle with.

It takes courage to have a conscience when you seem to see others getting something tangible out of not bothering to struggle with the morality of a situation. It gets frustrating and demoralizing. This is precisely where character comes in. All throughout history special people have felt compelled to do what they objectively saw as right and good—even in the face of humiliation or rejection or expulsion or torture or death. That is because they believed that certain ideas were more important than individual well-being.

BUT . . . THE OTHER GUYS WILL THINK I'M A WUSS

In our everyday lives, it's not unusual to have to face dramatic potential reprisals for our actions, even when we know they're right. That's where the challenge comes in. For Mark it was being considered a wuss by the guys.

Mark, thirty-one, is a stay-at-home dad of a five-year-old son since birth. He knows he's doing the right thing by his boy, but . . .

"I have kind of a problem," he said sounding embarrassed. "I've sacrificed so much in my career and it's been a financial nightmare, living hand-to-mouth. I wonder when the stress of it is going to end. It's worthwhile because I'm doing it for him. But I'm trying to get work and turning away jobs that interfere with my boy's schedule with me. It's difficult."

When I asked Mark if he wasn't getting some joy out of being there for his son, he eagerly told me, "I'm getting immense joy out of it!"

"Why, Mark, can't that joy be the end in itself?"

"Well, I guess," he pondered, "it's because the struggle is so hard. It's really great being with my son. I guess I look at my colleagues, you know, they're going to work every day."

"And, Mark, they're not able to have the relationship with their son that you have."

"Yeah, that's true."

"Be honest with me. Which situation would you rather be missing?"

"I'd rather be missing work, but . . ."

"Don't put a 'but' in there," I scolded him. "Mark, my man, you've got to be missing something, because life is a series of choices. When you drive to a corner you've got to pick one direction and proceed. You have to miss something to go somewhere."

"He's going to be starting school in the fall," Mark continued. "But I don't want to commit to any full-time job because I want to be there when he gets home from school."

"Wow, Mark, I just want to clone you."

"It's totally worth it. I was doing something and he was watching Power Rangers. I told him I needed some quiet and he went upstairs and he made this little card for me that said, 'Daddy, I love you,' and it was so touching. It's moments like that which make me realize work is nothing when you have that."

"And if you weren't there, Mark, that quality moment would have had no place in which to happen. Quality moments require quantity time in which to occur spontaneously. These other dudes going to full-time work every day will not have that memory. When you're about to die at 102 are you going to look back with regret about work or family?"

"Family," Mark admitted. "Nobody looks back at the work. I know. But you know how there is that pressure to compete and I have to make excuses about not meeting with someone because I have my son today."

"How 'bout having meetings at your house? Or, meetings brown-bagging it in the park while he's playing? Be creative! Instead of being apologetic, act proud!"

"Ohhh, Laura, that's great."

"Instead of saying 'I can't because'. . . say 'that's not good

for me because I want to be with my son, how about . . . ?'
Stop acting like a beaten puppy, act proud."

"I guess I needed a pep talk. Thank you."

Mark knew what he was doing was right. Yet, especially for
men, there is that competitive aspect of work, which is an
expected part of masculine life and identity. Mark's identity was
solidly situated with his parenthood role, but there were always
those lingering worries about the judgment of other men. I suggested he look at whatever negative reactions he got as "defensive envy," instead of a reasonable challenge to his choices.

You know, the general defensiveness about child-rearing,
especially from women, seems to be anchored in the "angry"
wing of the feminist movement. Having children and being
there to parent them has been maligned as a kind of cop-out
to the women's movement or a subjugation to a patriarchal
conspiracy to keep women from making money and having
political power.

Give me a break! When any movement or ideology
emphasizes rights as opposed to a balance of rights with
responsibilities, you know you have a destructive force in the
making. Now I'm going to give you a really powerful, personal example of what I mean.

In early 1994 with the release of my first book, *Ten Stupid
Things Women Do to Mess Up Their Lives*, I was booked for an
appearance on the *Donahue* show. One of the producers
informed me I'd be sharing the stage with five other women
whom I was to "help." Well, when they didn't put me on stage
until forty-five seconds before the camera went live, and there
was but one chair on the stage, I knew something had
changed. Boy, had it ever!

That book is about using courage combined with good
sense in making life decisions—i.e., taking responsibility and
healthier control over one's life. True to the sick and sad evolu-

tion of talk television, the thrust of the show was anything but that. Suddenly, I was confronting hostile questioning on hot-button issues like child care and spousal abuse that were only peripherally related to the book. The intention was to go to hyperbole to discount the usefulness of personal courage and responsibility in the face of supposedly insurmountable external conditions. Nonetheless, I managed to force it to come around to responsibility, and eventually the audience mostly came around to me!

When verbal grenades being lobbed at me about the impossible and outrageous notion of parent care for children in lieu of institutionalized day care got repetitive and annoying, I basically called a halt by challenging the entire audience with this question: "If you were going to wake up tomorrow morning as an infant, would you choose to be raised by a day-care center, nanny, or baby-sitter rather than by parents? If so, stand up now!"

Guess what? Nobody stood. Nobody even spoke. It was beautiful silence. I added, "Then don't do to your children what you wouldn't choose for yourself."

Incidentally, several people came up after the show to tell me the audience had been deliberately stacked and prodded to go after only controversial issues (TV is about ratings!). But that's aside from the point, which is that our society has gotten lazy and selfish and immature. There is too much pooh-poohing of responsible actions, planning and accepting consequences with honor.

BUT . . . ARE THERE REALLY OPTIONS?

Granted, you can find oases of nobility in this desert of parental self-interest. One such genuine noble soul wrote me a letter that touched me deeply:

I am a Resource Specialist in Learning Disabilities and work part-time (45 percent) for our local public school district, in order to have the most time for my three daughters, ages five, seven, and ten, and make ends meet at the same time. They are all in school now, but when they were younger, my husband and I worked opposite schedules in order to be home for our girls. We would meet off the freeway on our way to and from work, trading vehicles, and one went off to work and the other drove home with our girls.

I am the only person in my school district in my position working part-time. No matter how much pressure I've received from my employer to work full-time, I stay put because my husband and I strongly agree that our family comes first.

Unfortunately, in my position in the public school, I observe, daily, much to my dismay, the void left in the hearts and minds of children of all ages, including high school age children, when both parents work full-time and don't give the much needed time to their children.

I literally have junior high school students coming to me in tears begging me to help them with their homework and have lunch with them, because their parents virtually spend no time with them. These included students from so-called "good families" and families of my full-time colleagues!

My heart aches for children of dual full-time working parents, if only these parents could hear what I hear: their children saying, on a daily basis, like "My parents don't have time for me—they don't care," or "I don't even ask them for help anymore or even tell them when I get a good grade—they're too busy," or "My mom will get mad if the nurse calls her at work to tell her I'm sick."

Most gang members will tell you the reason they joined a gang was to have a "family" around them.

Or, as Melissa put it:

> So keep on speaking the truth about people who say they "don't have a choice about child care." They do; they just don't want it to seem that way. It gives their greed or misplaced values the appearance of nobility. Thanks for being a strong and reassuring voice for those of us who are making the hard decisions. Our kids would thank you too, if they knew any other way was even an option.

It amazes me that the concept of choice has become such an argumentative issue. You'd think people would be thrilled to acknowledge how much power they truly have to direct their lives. You'd think they'd revel in it. You'd think that, wouldn't you? Even our religious backgrounds acknowledge that.

When Adam and Eve were in the Garden they were not fully human because they made no choices between right and wrong, no value judgments, no issues of ethics or morality. Leaving Eden, though, meant becoming fully human, now having the capacity to choose to deny certain drives and cravings that are deemed improper or inappropriate.

Having the power to choose between good and evil is what makes human beings truly free. Our freedom consists of mastery over oneself, over our whims, temptations, immediate gratifications, self-centeredness, and greed, etc. That freedom to choose challenges us all the time.

And sometimes we don't like that.

Nancy, forty-seven, called all bent out of shape because her "fella" of six months turns out to be married. Her question was about whether or not it was right for her to tell his wife of the affair . . . mostly, I thought to punish him, and only somewhat to warn her.

That isn't the whole picture at all. I asked her if she'd been to his place of residence in the six months of their steamy sexual relationship: "No."

I asked her if she'd even been given his home number or spoke to him at home on the phone in the evenings: "No."

I suggested that she truly knew all along that he was probably living with someone, married or not, and that she ignored that because she didn't want to give up the immediate gratification: the passion and attention. Furthermore, she had a fantasy going that she'd get him.

She begrudgingly acknowledged I was right.

Frighteningly, she couldn't seem to get with the idea that what she did wasn't right. She was too busy displacing all the blame for the current state of affairs on his adultery, not her own lack of conscience in getting involved with an attached fellow (the impact on his partner/wife/kids) and her lack of courage in finding out truths up front and dealing with them. Motivation for this stupid behavior? Immediate gratification. She made a choice of "right now" over good sense or conscience.

Trying to avoid the self-examination, she calls to find out if it was right or not for her to blow the whistle on him. I told her, "That is a separate issue from what is my deeper concern about you, which is your denial that you made a choice, which got you to this point. If you tell on him, it doesn't change you, and you were not an innocent victim."

BUT . . . AWWW, YEAH, IT'S RIGHT

There's no denying that sometimes choosing to own up to your own weakness, badness, selfishness, or evil is tough to do. But it's the only way finally to get control and some peace of mind.

Sometimes the anonymous calls to my radio program are experienced as a kind of confessional—where folks can admit to errant thoughts and deeds, get some direction and support for facing themselves and fessin' up. The most dramatic of such conversations was with Henry, thirty-five.

"I'm one of those wicked, no-good people who molested a child some ten years ago. I'm trying to make amends today because I've tried to ignore it. At the time I was heavy into drugs and alcohol. I'm five years clean and sober. It was a thirteen-year-old girl, on about fifteen occasions. I was living with her mother for seven years, it was her daughter."

"Did the girl tell her mother or anyone else?" I inquired.

"I don't think so," he said quietly.

"Nobody ever filed charges against you?"

"No. But I don't know who's suffering more today, me or her."

"Trust me, she is."

When Henry agreed that was probably true, I advised him to turn himself into the authorities without resorting to plea bargaining and to make sure the girl and her family are made aware of his actions. That's important because, for many victims of sexual assault, a sense of finality only comes when justice is served. It's important to this girl, now a young woman, I counseled him, that there be consequences beyond his own remorseful, guilty feelings. Once Henry does the right thing, the girl will be freed from feeling bad about herself because the genuinely bad person got punished.

"Ironically, Henry, if you pay a price, you'll probably feel better and be able to let go. That means, both you and your victim will be helped. And, puhleese, don't go into excuses about how your past made you do it. Juries today just love that stuff, because on a personal level they imagine being off the hook for their bad deeds too. The truth is you chose to molest her to take care of your hurts, no matter how destructive that was to her, right?"

"What I did, I did of my own accord," he agreed. "I was just trying to get my own self-gratification. Whether I was loaded on drugs and booze is irrelevant."

"By the way, what did make a little girl attractive to you for sex?"

"She was just there. I just felt attracted. Her mom was a lot older than me. I never had any girlfriends growing up."

"So you had a mother figure, and a little girl who was not threatening because of her age, but she still had all the right body parts, right?"

"Right."

"I hope you are going to follow through with my recommendation. That way you could have a sense of peace and so will she."

"I'm going to. I just like to say to any guys thinking about doing what I did, for God's sake, don't! Stop. Stop. You've gotta stop. There is too much damage."

"Well, Henry," I signed off, "I never thought I'd ever say this to someone who has done what you've done, but bless you."

(Henry begins to cry.) "Thank you."

Henry's story highlights one of the most important reasons to do what's right; for peace of mind for you and others who might be victims of your misplaced energies. Think about it. This very moment, any moment, lasts but a moment. When you do something in that moment for the moment's worth of pleasure or to avoid discomfort, you live with the memory and the consequences of that moment for the rest of your life. If you have a conscience, you live also with the knowledge of what you've done to others. This is a poison with a long, long, half-life.

As we have seen already in this chapter, doing right is very challenging and there is rarely an immediate reward or reassurance. The reward for doing right is mostly an internal phenomenon: self-respect, dignity, integrity, and self-esteem.

Internal dignity, respect from others, and, as Charmaine writes, a life-style to be envied:

> Your program has confirmed how right I was in some major decisions in my life. I've done what was right, no matter how hard it was, initially, and have been called a fool. But those who have called me a fool are living chaotic, painful lives now, while I have a sense of order, calm, and peace. I just really appreciate your program.

Not doing right may have momentary payoffs but will wreak havoc with your self-esteem, respect from others, and quality of life. Think more seriously before you act without character, courage, or conscience. The rest of your life depends on what you do with any one moment.

4

Thinking "Poor Baby" Keeps You One
(Where's Your Self-Respect?)

I have something more to do than feel.
Charles Lamb

Want to know what I think about feelings? This letter from a listener, Becky J., sums up my attitude toward this subject:

> The most important message I've heard this year, and am practicing in my own life now, is to pay attention to what I "think," not always what I "feel"!
> My feelings were not always true to me, my thoughts are. There is a major difference between a thought and a feeling. My life works better for me when I pay attention to my thoughts and not so much my feelings. Thank you for pressing this point over and over again.

What heresy! Years and years of pop psych have taught us to construct a monument to our feelings; to make them the cornerstone of our identity and choice of behaviors; to accept all feelings as okay and meaningful; to operate as though (inner) feelings accurately portrayed (outer) reality.

I FEEL THIS WAY . . . NO . . .
I FEEL THAT WAY . . . NO . . .

Those notions get you in trouble every day, the kind of trouble that could lead to a lifelong predicament.

A young man called my program about his on-again off-again girlfriend situation of about one and a half years. They would emotionally react to each other (you know—get hurt, upset, angry, uncomfortable, frightened, etc.) and not follow up the feeling experience with clarification of what exactly transpired (objective description of circumstances) and how their unique reactions (subjective interpretations) combined to make a problem. And that, my friends, is what I really call a lack of communication.

Instead of communicating they would strike out. During one of those mad-at-each-other times, he had a quickie and the girl got pregnant. When he told his on/off girlfriend what had happened she was willing to take him back only if he had nothing to do with the girl and her baby. He was torn. He recognized his responsibility to this child in spite of having no real intimate relationship with its mother, yet he didn't want to lose his heartthrob.

"I feel so confused," he said. I asked him to answer one question in the general sense, philosophically instead of personally. I asked, "What do you think of a woman who wants her man to abandon his child for her sake?" He struggled with his feelings . . . and I challenged him to ignore his affectionate feelings for his girlfriend and simply answer the question from his mind. There was no longer a struggle for him. He responded quickly with, "Well, she'd be wrong." "Yes, I agree," I replied. "And," I continued, "do you believe that your love and need for your girlfriend, or hurt of the possible loss of her, should change that answer?" "No," he countered, firmly. "It's just that it hurts."

Yes, painful feelings do hurt. But the confusion we claim when we say that we don't know what to do because we're, for example, frightened of loss or negative judgment, is not true confusion. It is instead our longing not to have to give up any-thing we want (or believe we need), our longing not to have to feel anything unpleasant, our longing not to have to pay any price. Basically, by talking about "confusion" we try to avoid the necessity of mustering up the courage it takes to balance what we know and believe against primitive, self-protective, and often immature emotional reactions. Remember that feel-ings or emotions emanate from the more ancient, less evolved, lower part of the human brain, while thoughts are a product of our highly evolved, uniquely human, outer part of the brain.

WHY FORE ART THOU FEELINGS?

Are feelings useless, irrelevant, or stupid? Victoria asked this very question:

> **I have been listening to your program, and this is what I have learned:**
>
> **I do not make my decisions on the basis of my feelings.**

I do not determine my behaviors on the basis on my feelings.

I behave and decide on the basis of what is appropriate for me as a person with regard to my ethics, morals, intelligence, rights, discipline, commitments, goals, etc.

When I decide and behave on the basis of what is appropriate for the situation—that IS emotional maturity.

So here is where I am not getting it. I have realized the the "feels good–do it" philosophy is ultimately very painful. So, what is the purpose of having feelings? Why do I have feelings? Please let me know.

Well, Victoria, feelings are information that assists us, for example, in preservation as an individual (fear of a snarling bear makes you run/hide/defend self) and as a member of a group (shame makes us avoid behaviors that would lead to peer/community rejection).

Without using what I call "manual override"—that is, a rational second opinion (based on considerations of situation, knowledge, and experience)—your behavioral reactions to these feelings could be useless, irrelevant, stupid, dangerous, destructive, and sometimes even evil.

Simply put, running away and screaming for help when the above-mentioned bear is in a zoo cage is not too useful. Just going along with the peer pressure of a group using drugs to avoid rejection is stupidly self-destructive and worse if you prey on others as a result of the drug use.

Feelings are inner experiences, subjective emotional reactions, that are factored into making decisions about behaviors. They ought not be a simple, reflexive call to action. Those of you who use them as such often call yourselves sensitive. For example, from Frank: "I was talking with my AA sponsor, explaining that some of my behavior was motivated because I am 'sensitive.' It was quickly pointed out that I was 'immature,' not sensitive."

Immature? Immaturity masquerading as sensitivity believes that feelings fully represent reality. Immature emotional reactions are undiluted by pesky rational perspectives. Immaturity demands that the inner feeling world of the individual be the center of the universe and that the feelings of others are quite secondary.

Immaturity masquerading as sensitivity announces to others that they had best beware of what they say and do lest they upset you. If they even accidentally upset you, they are bad (simply because you feel hurt) and you are on a righteous course for vengeance: direct assault or manipulative whimpering.

Generally what sensitive people call communication is merely a highly energized (or woefully de-energized) vocalization, like a bear cub with a thorn in its foot calling for its mother. In fact, that's exactly what such sensitive communication expects: a completely compassionate reaction of licking and caretaking. Yet, even more is expected, isn't it? Namely, that the other person give up reasonable behaviors or their own emotional reactions. Your feelings rule.

FEELINGS AS BLUDGEONS

Actually, the fact that your feelings are hurt doesn't automatically imply the other person has done anything wrong. Barbara, forty, was about to discover this overwhelmingly difficult, yet simple truth.

"I'm separated from my husband for two months, he's

fifty-one, and it has been back and forth. We started dating again one week ago and the same old stuff just keeps happening. He gets his buttons pushed, I get my buttons pushed, we react in the same pattern, although I've done a lot of healing in this respect so I'm not as reactive in the same way. We raise voices, he becomes verbally abusive."

"Abusive?" I worried aloud.

"His voice is raised and he goes on and on."

"That sounds more annoying than abusive. Notice how you're using pop-psych terms: you go on less, so you're 'healed,' he goes on more, so he's 'abusive.' Maybe this name calling is part of your style of button pressing? If he were here now, how would he describe you? Be honest."

"He would describe me as being a very insecure person," Barbara replied.

"Is he wrong?"

"No, not totally," Barbara admitted.

"How would he describe you during these verbal tennis matches?"

"The real timid victim and the goody girl; I'm doing everything right and he's the bad guy," said Barbara.

"Have you ever told him that his rendition of your behavior is right?"

"No," she replied.

Refusing to stay an adult equal during disputes, Barbara resorts to "poor little hurt me" behaviors in the hopes that he'll just back off, stop arguing, and even caretake her. Instead, he roars with understandable frustration at her turnabout. She talks about herself as though she were a "healing" bruise, instead of someone who needs to change her nonconstructive behaviors. She talks about him as an "abusive" monster, instead of someone who is baited into aggravation. Up to here we have a no-win situation.

As Barbara and I probed further and she realized that the core of her defensive "I hurt—you're bad—now stop" approach to working out problems is that she was still insecure about having opinions and taking stands. She worried about rejection and, ironically, this worry led to behaviors that almost guaranteed rejection!

"I see that I've been operating under the rule of 'I hurt, you pay,'" Barbara acknowledged. "People have told me that my husband and I should separate because we just keep going over the same ground. He wants to work on it and says it'll be better. But I don't know how fast or how much I can change my insecurity part."

My suggestion was that although she may take at least some of her insecurity to the grave, she can immediately begin changing how she deals with it. Barbara knows full well when her insecurity gets tweaked—she could choose to deal with it internally by calming herself down, using positive, logical thoughts, giving herself reality checks, positive feedback, etc.; otherwise, she'd be making someone else responsible for her rather tenaciously protected personality trait.

In an emotional confrontation with another person, it's really essential to take time out to separate your irrational impulses from your rational thoughts. During that time ask yourself how much of what you're feeling is an appropriate reaction to the circumstances, and how much just has your ancient fears written all over it?

You see, the speed and effectiveness with which we apply reason to emotion is diminished when we refuse to surrender our power position of using hurt feelings to control or change others. Frankly, it's just hard to give up old habits, even when they don't work that well and we secretly know it.

When we're afraid to be strong, we use weakness to try to control others. We hope the weakness (the hurting, the pain, the "look what you've done to me"), will somehow preserve the relationship, whereas we fear that an appropriate use of strength (assertiveness) might cost us the relationship. The appropriate use of strength would only threaten a weak relationship with a weak partner. Maybe that's the knowledge you don't want to risk having.

A good example of irrational insecurity would be getting upset when a pretty woman or handsome man comes on the television screen; followed by your baiting and then berating your beloved about his or her appreciation of the sex symbol's attributes. Rational insecurity would occur after discovering that your beloved is actually two-timing you.

In the latter situation the tendency may be to try to preserve the fantasy of security in the relationship because losing hurts. It is at these times that you might prostrate yourself to win your lover back, hoping to inveigle them with sympathy, pity, or guilt. Forget it! Those emotions just aren't seductive, but they might leave you open to be used again.

Instead, realize that the loss may have more long-term benefits, including dignity and availability for life's potential personal growth and new, healthier relationships. That's when you need to use manual override of your natural instinct to maintain attachments, even lousy ones, and sustain yourself through the pain of loss and aloneness.

BUT . . . I NEVER WANT TO HURT AGAIN

Of course, if you're really determined not to get hurt ever again, you might simply sneak into a relationship and get what you want without giving too much, thereby minimizing your potential pain. That's what Dan, thirty-three and divorced, is doing.

Dan has been dating a widow, Noel, for eighteen months.

She has two children, both girls, twelve and eight. He said that he likes the kids a lot and loves Noel. However, he's afraid to get married. Why? Because he had an unfaithful wife, "So now I'm afraid of getting hurt again," he said.

I asked him if he'd been too afraid to have sex with Noel. "No," he said hesitatingly. I continued with, "Dan, have you been too afraid to spend time with the children and have them come to count on you?" "No," Dan replied again. "Dan, have you been too afraid to ask her to date only you and be sexually monogamous?" "No," repeated Dan. "Dan," I continued relentlessly, "have you been too afraid to enjoy her companionship and the feeling of 'family'?" "No," he said with resignation.

"So, the fear has been in the giving, not the taking," I concluded.

I told him he'd been so busy worrying about his potential hurt feelings that he hadn't noticed how self-centered and selfish he'd become. He hadn't even told Noel about not wanting to commit lest he get hurt or disappointed; he just kept taking and taking and taking.

"I'm . . . sort of shocked, Dr. Laura. I never thought about it that way."

"Dan, if you want to minimize the possibilities of getting hurt, I have recommendations. You need to take time to get to know Noel's character and something about her track record, her habits, and past excursions into inappropriate or inconsistent or immature behaviors. But I have to tell you that to avoid all possibility of hurt, you need to live in a cave or be in a coma. Otherwise, we all risk. That is our payment for our shot at life."

When we're preoccupied with our own needs, it's inevitable that we have less time, attention, and energy for others. We exist to take while being guarded about giving, urging others to display their vulnerability without reciprocating, reaping without sowing.

That was Dan's compromise, at someone else's expense, to avoid being alone.

BUT . . . WHAT IF I END UP ALONE?

So many folks would rather take direct hits of betrayal and abuse rather than exist even briefly without a someone. That's because, typically, they interpret being alone as a major negative assessment of themselves and an annihilation of hope.

Paul, a twenty-six-year-old gay man, recently discovered that his two-year live-in beloved is cruising via the Internet. That was only the latest in a too long list of examples proving the guy's lack of commitment to Paul. When I pressed Paul about losing this loser, he resisted with, "I'm afraid of being alone." Being an intelligent fellow, he realized that was objectively irrational—he wasn't going to die, develop terminal acne, or lose his job if he gave this fellow the heave-ho. So what was the fear really of?

"I was adopted, which I'm okay with. It's just that my adoptive father and I never really got along. All the time I was growing up he would yell and scream about how he wished I'd never been born, that I was useless, would not amount to anything, and so forth. There was rarely any peace or affection," Paul related.

Paul would try to form quick, not necessarily healthy associations and fight to keep them going, lest, through aloneness, he discovered that his father was right—he was not worth much to anybody. To Paul, aloneness equaled worthlessness, just like Daddy said.

The key element for Paul in continuing to suffer needless

hurt was that the struggle was wrapped in hope. Hope, therefore, would be lost with the loss of the relationship.

This is precisely where courage comes in; courage and your rational thought. The courage is necessary to suffer through the irrational thinking without letting it dictate behaviors, to learn to diagnose and analyze the situation through thoughts, not emotional reactions, and finally to struggle with new, healthier interpretations and actions that satisfy your rational mind without, for now, appeasing your emotions. This takes great courage.

MY PAIN, MY GAIN

Paul struggled to deny his father's mean condemnation of him by simply having a somebody in his life; if somebody was there, Dad was wrong. If nobody was there, Dad was right. Neat equation, simple solution, except that it trapped Paul into maintaining relationships regardless of their worthiness to him!

There is another way to deal with old pain and disappointment: have someone else make up for it . . . forever. This was Darcy's tactic.

"I've been in a relationship for seven months with a man who is very special to me. Unfortunately, I haven't always had success in my past relationships. About three or four weeks ago I was confused and a lot of hurt and anger from my past had come up, and he got the brunt of that and it hurt him very badly."

"What did he do, Darcy? How did he threaten you, intentionally or not, to cause you to bring in the wrath of your history and hit him over the head with it?"

"Well, nothing."

"Oh come on, Darcy. Maybe something he did or said

made you feel insecure, something got tweaked—what happened?"

"Well, maybe his attention was a little less."

"And so your emotional reaction was the fear that you'd be hurt, so your behavioral reaction was to dredge up all your old pain to say, 'You're responsible for never hurting me today because I had all this old pain'?"

While it is true that when a relationship starts to go bad there are some telltale traits—less attention, compassion, enthusiasm, consideration, etc.—it is also true that these traits may happen from time to time in healthy, ongoing relationships. People go through stressful times, the relationship goes through phases and challenges, the individuals come to be more open and honest about moods, needs, faults, thoughts, etc. Stuff happens, and so do temporary misbehaviors and misinterpreted actions.

Maturity allows us to sustain ourselves while investigating and discerning whether or not this is a temporary glitch or a seriously bad circumstance.

If we constantly overreact as though each glitch portends yet another apocalypse, then we don't allow the other person to be real, we refuse to acknowledge that relationships take work, we assume that the relationship must be a breast to feed only us.

"Dr. Laura," Darcy continued, "he's so hurt he is taking a break from me and the relationship. I don't know if it is for a while or what. He says he doesn't know. If our feelings were so strong for each other, how could he go?"

"Darcy, feelings can be very strong, yet decisions can be made not to stay in a relationship in which people see themselves as manipulated or made to feel totally responsible for the other's well-being and state of mind. That may be perceived as just too much of a burden. Assume this is permanent and challenge yourself to grow from it: to deal with the other person in the moment as equals. Others hurt too, Darcy."

The challenge is to learn something from our pasts, not to wear our pasts as protective warnings or as a victim's badge of honor. Time and again, people would come to me in my counseling office giving me coded warnings about their "sensitive" issues and areas. The warnings would take the form of stories about their past therapists, complete with their angers, hurts, and disappointments.

Interestingly, they would not be able to report having discussed these problems with their therapists—they'd just find a new one. When therapy got too difficult, challenging, or threatening, they'd leave and blame the therapist for messing up and hurting them in some way. This behavior is like keeping a skin wound festering and making sure no one ever touches that part of your body to hurt the hurt again.

We forget that scars and mended bones are stronger than the originals!

I'M HURT—NOW IT'S YOUR TURN

I realize that when we're hurt by someone or some situation, in addition to maybe licking our wounds and collecting sympathy, we obviously want to get out of pain as soon as possible. One of the least attractive ways we try to make that transition is with turning from the hurtee to the hurter.

Nancy, forty, was in an eleven-year long-distance, nonexclusive relationship. What's nifty about this is that you have intimate encounters without being overwhelmed by the perceived demands and threats of too much intimacy. This delicate balance was upset by a suggestion her boyfriend made.

"About a year ago he suggested that we might get together.

So, we talked a bit about getting closer, being monogamous. I agreed. This way of thinking didn't last long, he backed off and wouldn't even talk much to me for a while."

"Nancy, were you relieved, hurt, or a little of both?"

"Well, I only remember feeling hurt . . . and very angry."

"Your worst fears of getting close came true?"

"Maybe. But I was very angry."

"And then?"

"Well, it just happened. Last month I went out with his best friend and we slept together. My boyfriend found out about it and broke it off with me completely."

"Your attempt to give him some of the pain you got worked too well?"

"Well, I know I did something wrong, but look what he did!"

"Nancy, there are important, deep reasons people enter into these multiple loose liaisons, and they aren't to find the love of your life. They are to taste some of the riches of the earth without taking on the responsibility and work of creation and maintenance of the garden. These relationships survive as long as someone's worst fears aren't tweaked.

"Unfortunately, your fella tweaked you and you called his bluff about non-exclusivity by hitting too close to home. That tweaked him and he withdrew from the field of play."

"But, Dr. Laura, I don't understand why what I did was so bad—he hurt me first and I took it."

"You simply upped the stakes too high for him. But, perhaps more important for you, you used your hurt as a permission slip to hurt back. I realize you think that makes the score even so now you can start all over again, but you overestimated his capacity to use hurts, as you do, to justify safe emotional distance. The attack on his ego put him over the edge. And you lost."

Nancy's loss is one for which I, as a therapist, am grateful. If she doesn't obsess and try to harass and manipulate him back, she has the opportunity to open that door to intimacy wider and dare to walk through to greet someone with more openness and courage.

BUT . . . IT ISN'T FAIR

Using hurt as permission to hurt was also an issue with Tanya, twenty-seven. She's been in a two-year relationship with a fellow of twenty-five. After two years of using condoms they both went for HIV testing and were both negative. After mutually deciding on monogamy they gave up the condoms and . . .

"Now I have herpes!" she virtually screamed.

"Did he know he had herpes?"

"No, not really. He's only had a few mild occurrences and he never bothered to find out what they were. He just dismissed them as 'whatever,' because they went away.

"I'm thinking of getting out of the relationship. I find myself always angry with him, not only during my outbreak time, but because I have had to make lots of life-style changes to control it—you know, diet, stress, exercise, rest."

"What is his reaction, Tanya?"

"I don't think he's being understanding enough."

"How would he show you more understanding?"

"Good question. I don't know, really."

"Tanya, is it that he's had virtually no symptoms and you are suffering so much more than he that you resent his milder herpes case and need him to be sad and sympathetic all the time to make up for your pain?"

"Yeah, I guess so. I don't like that the suffering is mostly mine. I guess that's why I'm so critical of him—I want him to suffer more even though I realize he didn't do something on purpose to me. It was his ignorance. Nonetheless, it just isn't fair."

No, it isn't fair. Here is a young woman who tried to be careful. In life we must assume the risks for our activities and actions: if you play tennis you may sprain an ankle or get tendonitis—even if you've done the correct pre-match stretching exercises and use the best equipment. It hurts our sense of fairness and we want to strike out. It requires character to graciously accept these blows and be generous to those who escaped them.

And what about when the blows we have to absorb are set in motion by our own actions? Then, putting aside character and conscience, you might still claim victimhood. That is what Jim has done.

POOR ME . . . I HURT MY HAND HITTING YOU

Jim, thirty-eight, has been an alcoholic, closeted as much as possible, for over fourteen years, maybe longer. He's been married eight years and has two children, two and four years of age. His wife caught him drinking a couple of times and read him the riot act. Now he's owned up to her; he's admitted his drinking. He's in AA And, believe it or not, his feelings are hurt.

"My wife now has set new rules for the relationship. She would like to give it until the end of the year to see how I work out. Also, no sex and she's not physically supportive of me through this time. I know I've hurt her in every way that I could being the person that I am, and so these are her 'protected areas.' I'm not upset about it but it is really really hard for me because while I'm working in AA and researching what I've been and what I've done, the hard thing for me is that I go without the support system."

"Whoa, Jim, I think you're misunderstanding. You're not going without the support system. She's there for you. She's giving you the opportunity to straighten out. You're going without some of the behaviors of a healthy, intact relationship, such as lusty and loving sex, and perhaps lots of overt physical affection, but she has not abandoned you. Ultimately, she is still there. Your support system is being appropriately self-protective."

"Yes, that's right."

"But you are somewhat turning this around so that you almost look as if you are being victimized now. You're saying, 'Poor me, I'm not getting hugs. Of course, I messed with her mind and my family for years . . . but I'm not getting hugs!' "

"Right, that is right. Perhaps that's part of the 'poor me' stuff that I drank over."

It does diminish one's sense of being the transgressor, the bad guy, if you transform into some sort of victim. Now, someone else is the bad guy. Rather than manipulating his wife into the hugs and kisses and instant forgiveness and sense of normalcy in the relationship, Jim ought to earn them back by changing and growing.

"So, Dr. Laura, I have to eat dirt. But don't I have like, marital rights?"

"Baby, major dirt! And you'll be better for it. If you want to blow this marriage and family right now start jumpin' up and down proclaiming your conjugal rights no matter what you've done. She's a woman with two babies who is worrying that she might not have a man and a marriage because he might pick the bottle over her. That doesn't make anybody feel sexy or even affectionate."

"It's just hard on me too."

"So it's hard on you. Nothing has been done to you, Jim, not by your wife, some stranger, or deus ex machina. What you're reaping from her is what you have sown. She didn't get up one morning and decide to cut off sex to torture you. Instead of bemoaning that you're not getting your goodies you should be thrilled out of your mind, grateful that she didn't abandon you. Share that feeling of gratitude with her."

Jim's centered-around-the-self attitude—and his counting the spaghetti strands not on his plate—are part of the dynamics of drinking for many people. He's not a man entirely without conscience. He realizes and doesn't deny or diminish the hurt he's caused. However, he disconnects from the other person's hurt, and the consequences wrought by causing them pain, by continuing to demand his due, as though his pleasure should exist even in the vacuum he's created.

This self-centered version of life is not very rewarding, yet some hold on to it with a vengeance—an ugly vengeance.

TO SAVE YOU FROM HURT
I'M GOING TO HURT YOU FIRST

Even after waiting on hold for forty minutes, Caroline, fifty-two, came on the line sniffling and began her dialogue with me with an ever increasing intensity of tears. I asked her to take a breath so that I could understand her. With twenty years of others' tears under my belt, I feel I can usually judge tears of fear, embarrassment, pain, and self-pity or poor me. These were definitely "poor me" tears.

"I'm so terribly upset. I haven't talked to my son for almost a year and then I got an invitation to his wedding, which is tomorrow. I'm really so very hurt. I just don't know what to do about this wedding."

"How is it that you haven't been in communication with him for so long?"

Caroline continued in martyred tones, "I just want the best for him and he's just asking for so much trouble and so many problems. He's marrying someone of another culture. I told him . . ."

"Some other culture?" I queried.

"He was in Colombia for two years doing missionary work. That's where he met her. She was there also doing missionary work."

"But what are you so hurt about?"

"That he has chosen to ignore my warnings about the trouble he'll have in his life marrying someone from another culture."

"Let me get this straight. You're worried about him being hurt by the bad, bigoted behavior of strangers so you're getting him used to it in advance by giving it to him yourself?"

"I'm not bigoted," she said with irritation. "I just want him to be happy."

"You want him to be happy so you give him grief rather than stand by him as he honors his loving commitment to his beloved? It would be that difficult for you to hug her and be gracious?"

"I think so, I just don't like it. This is causing me so much pain."

"Excuse me? Nobody is doing anything to you. Your son, an obviously good and unselfish person, has met his match. If indeed he is going to suffer some from people who are into ethnic purity, it is your job as a good mother to support and reinforce him. The problem is that in this case, his mother is part of the enemy. The only perpetrator of pain here is you. By the way, you should be grateful that your son didn't inherit your lack of tolerance."

Bottom line is that when parents rebel against the individuality of their children, as though it were intended to be a personal slap instead of an adult choice, parents have to choose between "their way" and "go away." I asked Caroline if she wanted to be in her grandchildren's lives or preserve her son from further hurt by keeping out of his life. Guess what she chose!

Caroline's problem is part of a syndrome I call "There Shalt Be No Feelings Before Mine." People with this syndrome inevitably express themselves with words suggesting caring and generosity, but with an undertone hinting at hostility below the surface. And the last approach they're prepared to take is introspection.

LIKE IT . . . OR ELSE

A twist on "no feelings before mine" is when you discount the feelings of others under your rule—that if you don't agree with their feelings, or if their feelings don't make sense to you, their feelings have no validity. I'm convinced that most of the time this is the result of defensiveness: perhaps you've done or said something hurtful and are uncomfortable reaping the consequences, so you tell them they shouldn't feel that way because they are "too sensitive" or that you "didn't mean it the way it was taken." Well, they just might be sensitive in that area—still, that doesn't absolve you of responsibility for aiming there again and again. And just maybe you did have some ambivalence in your intent, perhaps part of you did mean to make a camouflaged strike. Then, owning up, talking it through, and resolving the problems is the best remedy.

Kay Lynn's call highlighted this issue. To give her husband a fifty-fifth birthday gift, she'd taken the only three small diamonds he'd given her on their engagement and their first and fifth anniversaries and had them set in his wedding band. Unfortunately, he reacted with shock and anger. Kay Lynn said she was completely surprised by his response.

I suggested that perhaps on his fifty-fifth birthday, he didn't want a gift that may symbolize to him a lack of accomplishment, i.e., his wife had to recycle his presents to her in order to give him something.

"I understand that . . . I just don't agree with it."

"Well, Kay Lynn, you don't have to agree with someone's feelings and point of view to behave respectfully given those realities. I don't get the impression that you are unwilling to understand his feelings."

"I don't, that's right, because that was such a sacrifice for me."

"It may be that fact which embarrasses and hurts him so much—that you had to sacrifice. It may make him feel like a failure, even if you don't mean to convey that message. Perhaps he would have enjoyed a night out with you, some special family event—all of which would highlight his meaningfulness as husband, father, man."

Kay Lynn really didn't want to hear any of this. She was into how her sacrifice wasn't being heralded. I wondered if she didn't really mean to hurt him with this sacrifice, to express mostly contained frustration at what they didn't have in things. While I can understand disappointment at having generosity met with displeasure, to which I would expect disappointment, she was completely unwilling to acknowledge his hurts.

Quite frankly, a determined, complete blackout of the acceptance and meaning of the other's hurts usually tips me off to an exaggerated attempt to deny that you indeed did, even in a small way, want to hurt them.

WHAT DID YOU MEAN BY THAT?

Except for feelings like compassion and altruism, much of what we recognize as feelings keeps us focused inward. That can become a habit, especially when we're trying to protect our self-image. It is amazing how we will protect it in one arena and blow it completely in another.

Judy, forty-five, has a problem with anger. Interestingly, when someone hurts her feelings she does everything she can not to show anger. Later, she takes that simmering anger and dumps it on someone safe, like her for-better-or-worse dear husband.

"I know I should simply address what is going on with the problem when it first occurs. I know it's not nice to hurt my husband with my hurts," Judy admitted.

It would seem obvious that the solution is to be assertive, courageous, and communicative at the moment, even though confrontation is threatening and upsetting. So why didn't I recommend this course of action? Because the comments that hurt her were right on target.

Those supposedly "hurtful" comments were about her weight. Many co-workers and friends were apparently worried that her thinness indicated an eating disorder. Not wanting to face this possibility, she would not enter into a confrontation. Instead, she would take her hurt home and clobber her husband—this rageful outlet made her feel "bigger" again.

IT AIN'T PERSONAL

There are those who take things much too personally because they are vigilant guardians of the smaller picture (self) instead of the bigger picture (others, the relationship, the particular situation, and/or even the truth).

Kim, thirty-two, called because she had had a bad Saturday night. She jokingly told me that in her mind she'd had an hour-long conversation with me at three in the morning.

"It's concerning my daughter, one and a half. A year ago I sat down with my sister and her husband and we all agreed that she'd become the guardian of our daughter if something happened to me and my husband. She agreed, and I've been happy about that. When I spoke to my cousin last Saturday, who has a daughter six months old, he announced to me that he and his wife had asked my sister to be the guardian of their child should they croak. That my sister hadn't mentioned anything about it is upsetting to me."

"Which upsets you more profoundly—that your sister didn't mention it or that she is to be the guardian of someone else's kid?"

"I'm sort of resentful that my cousin squeezed in on the little bit of family that I have that could take that responsibility. I also felt that with my sister not saying anything to me and with accepting so much responsibility that my child would get less in the event she was needed."

"Wait a minute, Kim, does the fact that you and your cousin both value your sister's responsibility and lovingness, and that she agreed to be available to both, make you feel less special?"

"Yeah, that's true."

"So, you wanted to have this special relationship with your sister. That it now seems as if she has a business servicing the children of dead relatives makes it less a bonding experience and more an estate-planning experience?"

"Yeah, it just doesn't feel as . . . as special. And I don't like the idea of my sister's attention being subdivided if she's taking care of my daughter."

"You think your daughter will only get the necessary love and affection if there are no other kids around?"

It's interesting how confused we get. Kim bemoans her lack of extended family, hence her wanting first and only dibs on her sister, yet underestimates the benevolent impact of more kids in her sister's home (should everyone all die in unison) for family bonding.

I asked Kim, "If you had three kids and one of them came to you and said, 'I think you love me less and I'm not special because you also love the other two,' what would your answer be?"

"I'd say, 'That's not true. The more of you I have, the more I love. I love you as yourself.' "

"And, Kim, maybe your sister loves you for yourself and she doesn't need to keep you as the 'only one' to feel that love and to give you that love."

"Okay, I got it."

The mathematics of how Kim had been feeling before is called the Null Sum Hypothesis; that is, there is a certain amount of everything, like love, and if someone gets more, you get less. This makes for competitive, hoarding behaviors. If someone else gets something, you are automatically hurt by your feeling of entitlement or the threat of loss. Talk about synthesizing your own hurt!

In all fairness, if it involves you, no matter what, it's bound to tweak you somehow. The trick is then to figure out how to know when to go to war or not, when to feel hurt or angry or not.

IT AIN'T PERSONAL, IT'S ONLY BUSINESS

Carolyn, thirty-one, is an airport traffic police officer. Yeah, one of those authority figures who tells you to move on even though you've given them some cock-and-bull story about how it'll just be a minute. People give her "lots of crap" and she's having trouble resisting the urge to pull her gun when men and women alike shout epithets and nasty comments. She's being worn down by the aggravation.

This is one of those times we've got to realize that she's dealing with folks who are tired, frustrated, inconvenienced, self-centered, and ill-mannered. Therefore, it isn't about her capabilities as an officer. The travelers just don't want to consider the welfare of others when they're tired and want to go home or frenzied about the long lines, delays, and heavy baggage.

I suggested that in response to these people, she ought to restate the obvious. For example, "I can see you've got a lot of luggage and it would be easier to park here in the nonloading zone, and I'd be delighted to let you if there were no other passengers around in the same position—believe me I would. Now, the fastest and easiest and most convenient parking for unloading is . . ."

Stating the obvious, acknowledging the position and potential feelings of someone else, takes away a lot of the other's fire. Feeling acknowledged and understood is a great sedative to rage and anxiety. Yet, you are not giving up on your position. You are just using a tool that more likely gets the other person more in gear to follow your guidelines.

This position is a professional stance that gives you personal emotional distance from taking any of the crap as personal. Compensatory activities, like warm baths and increased interaction with the more polite customers, also alleviates the stress.

Even when you aren't a professional, or in a professional circumstance, you can bring thoughtful, rational discourse into situations you'd normally get crazy over. However, one of the reasons we don't handle things rationally is because we either are or feel incompetent to do so.

It may be difficult to imagine that someone's discomfort or disagreement with anything, from our religion or politics, to living arrangements and hair color, isn't personal . . . but it doesn't have to be taken as such. Sometimes we react with emotion because we don't feel strong, informed, or capable enough of presenting our side. Therefore, we simply resort to acting hurt rather than explore the issues. Perhaps that's because it would tickle our own doubts, reveal our own limited knowledge, and cause us to question areas that would threaten our immediate security.

In other words, we get hurt rather than introspective.

What makes introspection so scary? Probably because it leads us into internal emotional areas of which we're just too scared. It becomes easier to transpose hurts—trading or substituting one easier dealt with feeling for another, much more threatening feeling. We accept experiencing a feeling we can more readily survive to defend against a deeper, more meaningful, therefore more potentially devastating, feeling. That idea brings me directly to Mike.

HIDE-AND-SEEK WITH MYSELF

Mike, twenty-five, has a repetitive behavior he says he can't seem to stop. I asked him not to tell me the exact behavior just yet, and actually, we never got to it. The actions were of less importance than the motivating feelings hidden behind the behaviors.

Mike admitted to feeling better after he'd done "whatever it was he was doing" and to "experiencing an irresistable need" when he tried to resist.

"Temporarily, right? You only feel better temporarily after you've done it?"

"Yes, temporarily."

"Or one time would be enough."

"Yes, exactly. Then it's over and I don't feel good about myself any longer. Another pressure is the acceptance from my group."

"Therefore, you want a quick fix to how badly you're feeling about life or yourself; and you want to fit in. This discomfort provides a requirement for a solution, therefore you designate a certain inappropriate action as the solution. The end result is that you don't feel better for long."

"That sounds terrible, but it's right, Dr. Laura."

"Philosophically, the issue is that you cater to the need (the quick-fix behavior) because you are unwilling to tolerate some other, very important discomfort? You're willing to sell out the greater good of well-being as a person to feel better right now ... like a drug addict. And you sacrifice your integrity to 'fit in.' The pain of recognizing that you've gone against your grain is not as painful as the pain you avoid. How can you ever get better unless you're willing to tolerate that pain? Which means when the need comes you tolerate not feeling good right now. I need you to suffer, babe."

Mike laughed. "All right. There are those times of loneliness and self-doubt that I bury with the quick-fix behavior. I need to learn to tolerate those moments."

"Mike, powerful feelings like loneliness or self-doubt are universal and are just the price of living without arrogance. These powerful feelings are sometimes indicators that we need to change some attitude or direction. How can the message they're trying to give us be dealt with constructively if we simply try to erase them? Dealing constructively requires the character implicit in discipline."

"It would be easier if I just ..." or "Just one more time," or even "What the hell, what's the difference anyway" are some of the many meaningless spontaneous rationalizations we use to avoid pain. And, the pain of needing to "fit in" or "feel good" or "feel alive" right now is quite seductive. This is where courage and patience come in—or so-called addictive behaviors walk in instead.

BRING BACK THE BAD OLD DAYS

Destructive behaviors are not the only way to try to avoid a deeper pain. Escaping into yesterday will also work for some. Steve, twenty, finds himself inexplicably festering over the old pain of a lost relationship with a girlfriend. One and a half years ago, while he was a teenager, he was going with a girl for two and a half years, who broke off with him to go off with his best friend. Two losses simultaneously.

He called because it was all coming back up in his conscious mind again after he thought it was over and dealt with. He was thinking about it, and hurting over it, all over again.

"Steve, why do you think this is coming up now? Why not a year ago? What is unique about now?"

"Well, I recently moved to new area, I'm far away from everybody. I don't have close friends at this moment. I'm planning to start a new school. I feel a need for friendship."

"You are taking the next step into adulthood. You realize you are on your own and you are perhaps overwhelmed with the unfamiliarity of your circumstance between where you live and a new school. It is natural to want to make the unfamiliar familiar. You can do that by working directly on forming new attachments and routines—or you can reach backward for memories of a time it was more comfortable for you. This is not likely to be about your continued love for her, certainly you neither respect nor admire her behaviors. This is about trying desperately to reconstruct a time in which you felt connected and safer."

One of the things we do when we're scared to death of the new is that we refocus in on the old—the nostalgia for a time that "worked." We, of course, don't want to admit we're scared to death. That's more difficult than saying, "My heart yearns for her." So we dump the scared feelings and obsess about "her" and how it was then. Whew! No more fear! Oh yeah?

Well, if we don't anesthetize the fearful feelings with compulsive behaviors, stretching into the past, what else can we do to jump off the reality ship? Among other tactics, we can project our feelings onto someone else and urge them to deal with it. Ginger will tell you all about that.

DON'T LOOK AT ME, MY MOM NEEDS HELP

Ginger, twenty-three, called because she was fretting over her mom.

"I have a feeling my mother is in real need of psychological help because she is assuming my marriage will break apart because of what has happened to her. I've been married three years, he's twenty-two, we have two children, two months and sixteen months."

"Objectively, what is there about your marriage your mother might have concern with?"

"Because my husband and I fight; no matter where we are we discuss it right there and get it over with. She has a hard time with that."

"Frankly, most people would be uncomfortable with that. You don't use any discretion or self-containment to wait to a private time—you'll do it no matter who is around?"

"Well no, only family. Not in public. The thing I'm worried about . . . my mother was divorced when I was twelve. And when they were married they never argued, never fought."

"So could the reason you spontaneously take on any and all hurt feelings to counteract the notion your parents had that there should never be fights? That oversimplifies relationships—fighting in front of family doesn't insure a long-term marriage. That is what your mother is reacting to, and in fairness, we shouldn't discount her as a flake-pot because she did the opposite of you and ended up divorced."

I'm against dealing with hurt feelings the millisecond your being recognizes one. A lot of people think that because they feel hurt they are justified in feeling hurt. Simply because you have a hurt feeling doesn't mean that the other individual actually did anything bad. It could be that you have an interpretation or association between his action or word and something negative. But, you see, that has nothing to do with him or his intent.

When you react immediately, you don't give yourself the time to explore that and to get a rational grip on the feeling. If you did you could discount it as inappropriate to what happened and dismiss it, or choose to talk about your unique reaction or perception based on your personal experience. All in all, you must take responsibility for the reaction and not blame the other person or make him feel uncomfortably and inappropriately guilty.

To reiterate, not every hurt feeling needs discussion. For two people to survive a long-term relationship they've both got to pick battles and not react as if every mood, joke, and comment were a personal assault or a threat to the relationship. Some things are important (talk about those), and some things simply need to be let go of (assessed as benign in the generally positive context of relationship). Something that is repetitively insensitive and destructive needs to be dealt with.

Whoa! There it is, the threat of dealing with something you'd sooner swig castor oil than face. Among the defensive techniques tailored for such avoidance is, for example, turning your fears and insecurities into anger at some innocent party as if a change in his or her current actions would magically rewrite our history or change the fact that we need to get a grip on our own lives.

BUT . . . WHAT ABOUT ME?

Thirty-two-year-old Liz says she is really angry. Liz is separated with three children under eleven. The object of her rage is Phil, recently divorced with two children under four. She feels he spends too much extra time with his kids, beyond what visitation calls for. She rationalizes her complaint by telling Phil that his behavior "will only serve to confuse your children and give them false hopes."

Imagine, a woman complaining that a man wants to spend tons of time with his kids! I guess it would be all right if that time were with her kids, and if he were her ex-to-be?

Liz's real issues are with the abandonment and rejection feelings from her ongoing separation and divorce, in addition to her fears of being alone. Character sometimes gets pushed aside when fear enters the picture. Liz is scared to be on her own with the awesome responsibilities of a single parent—that's understandable. Her anger at having to feel fear and insecurity is now directed at Phil—she imagines that if he wouldn't spend so much time with his kids she'd feel better about everything.

That's projecting responsibility for one's own life onto somebody else, without regard to who else, what innocent, would have to pay the price. She'd rather see his kids have the legal amount of his time, not a moment extra, so she would be saved. So much for character, courage, and conscience.

Instead, she needs to get more concrete about how to face the challenges of a divorced single mom and develop the skills necessary and the support system that would be helpful. This isn't the easier way—it's just the healthier way.

I KNOW YOU LOVE ME . . . RIGHT?

Unfortunately, although "easier" is too often the chosen criterion for a course of action and emotion, it rarely gets the job done. Penny, thirty-one, is happily married with a two-year-old daughter. She's going to Wisconsin, with the child and husband to follow, to celebrate her daughter's birthday with her folks and is feeling nervous. She worries that her dad is not really interested in her because he doesn't sit her down and ask about every detail like Mom.

"Penny, perhaps he feels questioning you would be nosy, intrusive, and too parental, and imagines if there were something you want him to know you'd tell him. That's an alternative to 'not interested in your life.' Fathers don't act like mothers all the time, you know. Maybe he's interpreting your non-forthright behavior as you not being interested in sharing your particulars with him. You are putting evil intent onto his behaviors. If you look at your dad objectively, do you think he shows caring?"

"Oh, I know he cares," Penny said emphatically.

"Why does he have to do it one specific way in order for you to give him credit for it, the caring?"

"It's easier."

"It certainly is difficult to get out of the child mode into co-adult mode with our parents, even after we become parents ourselves. You want to know he cares. You know he cares. But the little girl part of you doesn't want to find out he doesn't. That's the part that made the rule: Questioning equals Caring. That's easier than asking, or finally simply accepting the caring without all the renewals."

"Yes, that makes sense. I guess I've been hurting my own feelings with my interpretation. It's just that with the distance between us and the few times we get to be together I want to know I still matter. That I'm still his little girl."

If every time Penny chatted with her dad about "what's going on," he ran out of the room gagging, or promptly fell asleep, she might have a case. We all have formulas for how certain interactions should be or how somebody should show a particular sentiment. We end up being frustrated, disappointed, and hurt a lot through our own misinterpretations. We need to do reality checks—that is, ask.

Part of our emotional expedition into adulthood is to stop using our parents as assumed perpetrators of all our pain, most of which turns out to be self-inflicted after all. This seems so obvious—so why is it so difficult to do? For some people, sad and painful feelings, or rage about those feelings, become their identity, not to be given up easily.

BUT I'M THE GOOD KID

Darlene, thirty-three, is a perfect case in point. Admittedly, it's wonderful when your parents reflect the best of your own best self-assessment, but how many times do they have to do that for you to continue to be okay? Who else are they expected to abandon or put down in order to avoid all comparisons and competitions so you won't feel diminished, therefore hurt?

"My brother is a total bum," Darlene announced irately. "He uses drugs. He has no responsibilities whatsoever and my parents support him; he is living with them. It has always been that way."

"So I'm sure you wonder why the bad kid seems to get rewards and the good kid flies on her own?"

"Yeah."

"Well, you can get what he's getting—just go on drugs and drop out. To me, that seems like an awfully big price to pay."

"I don't really want that."

I pointed out to Darlene that she was looking at the situation backward: as if he were being rewarded by their parents for being a bum. That was wrong, because what reward is it to ultimately have nothing, do nothing, be nothing? He's helpless, dependent, and without prospects. Their parents keep him alive . . . hoping.

It was when I called her on her jealousy, in its distorted form, that she got heated.

"I don't envy him."

"Darlene, I think you do. I think you envy the attention and assistance and seeming support when you've worked so hard on your own. And you've gotten the payoff. You're independent, happily married, a mother, successful, competent, have a good life. That's your reward. You're wasting some of the joy of the rewards of your efforts in worrying about your bum of a brother who lives with your folks only because they're scared he'll die on the streets. Of course, there are some better things they could be doing to help him for the future— but they're focused in on right now."

"Then why is it that they were always hard on me?"

"I don't know that they were hard on you, but they probably knew you 'had it' and they pushed you to keep it and use it. They knew he couldn't take it because he's not as strong and that he wouldn't do it. They gave up with him, sadly. They are now running on guilt. You can't envy what comes from not doing well."

"But doing okay is so difficult."

"Yes, it's easier to obsess about your brother who seemingly has it easier; just like it's easier for your brother to do drugs. If your brother were dead tomorrow it wouldn't make life easier for you."

"How do I handle all this rage, this feeling that my parents abandoned me or care about him more?"

"By realizing that it isn't rage; it's fear of all the things you have to face on your own—and you are angry you have to. But, Darlene, we all do."

"Oh God, that's right. I didn't think about it like that."

Suzanne, thirty, drives the point home:

"I have been angry toward everyone because I haven't had it so good or easy. I have been internalizing this anger and passing it on to my boyfriend. I have always admired him for pursuing what he loves, and now suddenly I'm resentful. I've been playing poor pitiful me and have slacked off at work using any excuse in the book. I've finally examined myself, my goals and true passions. I've always wanted to be a therapist, but never wanted to deal with entrance exams, studying, and, quite honestly, my own fears. I know I have the power to achieve what I dream when I face my fears and risk change; no guts no glory!"

Here again, as with Darlene, a kind of comparative, competitive obsessing and rage betray a deeper fear of new challenges. The substitution of hurt feelings for hard work. Interesting use of feelings, don't you agree?

Life is a challenge, sometimes it seems a slalom, an obstacle course, a trial by fires, even a bad joke with you as the subject. I don't believe for a minute that everything that happens to you is your doing or your fault. But I do believe the ultimate quality of your life, and your happiness, is determined by your courageous and ethical choices, and your overall attitude.

In other words, you may get shipped some bad bricks and weak steel, but you are still the general contractor who decides what to do about it. What do you want to do? Fake it? Bemoan it? Change the plans? Wait for better parts?

Because this process is difficult, many find ways of avoiding taking on the task. One of many ways to do that is to exaggerate the problem even more . . . in so doing, overwhelm yourself out of the process of even trying to cope.

GIVE ME THIS DAY MY DAILY MOLEHILL

Diane, thirty-nine, chooses to do this by making, in her words, "mountains out of molehills." She thinks about a problem so much that by the time she confronts the person or situation, it's graduated to a crisis so powerful that it's impossible to deal with.

"Do you withdraw or get real mean?"

"Both. But I'm driving myself crazy about everything— my looks, brains, judgment . . . I guess I'm just insecure."

"Insecure sometimes means that you haven't done the things you need to do so that your reputation with yourself has grown."

"Right. I kind of avoid confrontations or situations where I could fail or feel bad."

"Diane, everybody's feelings are hurt when they hear negativity. The task becomes to sort out the usefulness of the hurtful information. We do that by getting more than one opinion. We do that by measuring the input against the yardstick of our own earned self-assessment."

Basically, Diane makes it worse as an attempt to avoid dealing with it concretely. Self-examination, the challenge of personal growth, is being cleverly bypassed.

I would see this maneuver in therapy sessions with couples. One spouse would voice a concern, description of behavior, or complaint about the other spouse. The reaction would be the most gross exaggeration of what was heard, in fact to the point of being ridiculous, in order to squeeze out from under it. For example: "I was uncomfortable with how you behaved at the dinner party" is responded to with, "There you go again, always complaining about my behavior . . . everything I do is wrong . . . I never meet your criteria," etc., instead of owning up to the transgression and being done with it. But no. You don't want to look bad or admit to being bad.

Naturally then, time is spent fixing the "perception" before you can get to the avoided issue of the original complaint. In addition, the process of fixing the perception causes one to have to say things that makes the transgressor not look or feel so bad, right? Things like, "Yes, I know it isn't ALL the time," or "Yes, I realize you have sometimes been nice to them," etc. Clever.

Exaggerating complaints to avoid taking responsibility is a self-defense technique. Take this a step further and you have an individual whose virtual identity is as the "hurt one." In a commentary about Burt Reynolds entitled, "Pain, Anger Stir Reynolds' Demons" in the *Los Angeles Daily News* (10/25/94), Phil Rosenthal wrote about this kind of problem: "They show us a chip with a man attached at the shoulder, angrily grasping for something from which anger can only separate him. Life is not a zero-sum game. Opponents, real or perceived, don't have to lose in order for a person to win. Misery is to be overcome, not passed on."

Alex, thirty-eight, is struggling with this lesson. Alex's girlfriend says that he's always nurturing misery. He admits to being hurt or sad a lot. He says he grew up angry and is still angry. He says that his mom always treated him differently from the other kids. I suggested to him that she may, at least in part, have reacted to unique qualities of his personality, demeanor, and behavior.

So many people imagine they're born devoid of individual traits. They believe that everything they are is because of what happened to them. Two things are ignored in this regard: first, that they were born with certain characteristics of temperament and behavior to which others respond uniquely, and second, that incidents are not as important as our take, or perception, of the meaning of the incident. That latter experience is also unique to each individual.

"Basically, I've grown up a very angry person. I realize it is a problem. My girlfriend says my misery is going to break us up and I realize that she is a very outgoing and energetic person and this is not good for her."

Anger can be used as one of those protective devices—a kind of armor. It is often invoked instead of being open, courageous, and honest with others and situations.

"Alex, you say 'angry,' she says 'misery.' Is the anger your defense against the feelings of misery?"

"Probably. I know I have a problem. I've been in counseling. I've learned I have to let go of my childhood. I'm angry with my mom and all my brothers and sisters—my dad left when I was three."

"How did your mom treat you that was bad?"

"She told me I was lazy and good for nothing."

"Were you lazy?"

"I guess, yes. I liked to sit and read and write alone."

"It looks as if you've taken some things your mom has said and done as an indictment of you, and you're leading your life too scared to find out she's right. Here's another rendition: your mother is a young woman with a bunch of kids who's just been abandoned by her husband. This automatically puts stress on her and the family. With this much pressure, she's going to be less likely to be patient with what she perceives as weakness or laziness. If this were a two-parent family, then your more quiet, laid-back, slightly fearful or timid personality style could have been more positively approached.

"This is different than evil intent, don't you think? When we think about 'what was,' we don't have VCR-quality memories, nor do we appreciate what we as infants and small children brought into the situation by virtue of our innate personalities, nor can we appreciate the objective nature of the situation. As children we naturally personalize. As adults we have the privilege of objectivity. This is not to shift 'blame' from Mom to you—so that now you can be angry with yourself, or completely exonerate your mom. This is to show that perhaps there is no blame. Maybe that's more frustrating because it leaves you with no target to complain about when life doesn't go well. It leaves you having to face up to, and attempt to develop, your own limitations."

Alex felt deficient because he wasn't able to be happy all of the time, he didn't always feel in control or able to snap himself out of feelings of insecurity or a glitch in confidence, and he wasn't immediately aware of how to deal with some challenging situation. Frankly, that is actually all normal to the human experience. It is true that the early loss of his dad and the obvious pressures in the family may have compounded Alex's sensitivities. It is also true that finding blame does not find solutions—the natural end point for that path is false self-gratification: I'm not bad/weak/frightened, etc., I'm a victim.

I suggested that he give himself permission not to have to work his way out of this because of his "suffering." He enthusiastically agreed, believe it or not! He responded with, "It's like I live for misery, it's my identity, it's who I am," instead of being "lazy" or frightened.

How to stop? Here is where we need to create a big divide between feelings and behaviors. Once we have recognized that the feelings are reflexive and irrational, it becomes important to decide concretely that one's behaviors will not be dictated by those feelings.

For example, Alex mentioned that if his girlfriend went to play a baseball game instead of going out with him to a movie, his reaction would be to "feel rejected." Exactly! Therefore, he would say to her, "You don't like me." That's the point at which we realize that we see the world and others only through our own needs. Instead, Alex could stuff those "irrational" and self-centered feelings and say, "I'm going to bring some popcorn and be your best cheerleader!"

Inside Alex could still be nurturing poor-me feelings of rejection, because that doesn't change as fast as behaviors. When we change our behaviors to the positive, it drags our feelings into the positives of growth, development, and maturity. Because you are doing what you intellectually know is right, and you are getting great feedback for being giving as opposed to suffering.

Ultimately, we all need to survive the reality that each day is mixed with pleasure and pain. We don't need to react to each pain by the self-defensive mode of saying, "See? The world is miserable to ME." We need to reach to each pain by either waiting it out, adjusting, or addressing it directly. It's scary, I know. It's difficult, I know that too. But it gives you the best chance at overall pride.

The dependency Alex described with his girlfriend is to solicit the mothering and fathering he missed. In healthy relationships we, in part, do reciprocal positive parental nurturing. But one-sided parenting or childing indicates an unhealthy relationship.

It is tempting to believe that the world owes us because of our losses and hurts, in which case our eternal suffering is our technique to insure caretaking. We might exaggerate, distort, or misinterpret the actions of others, as a warning to them about their being more careful about our "hurty" places. We are trying desperately to avoid hurt—but with this mind set, hurt is all we ever feel.

HELL NO, I WON'T LET GO

Hurt is also all we ever feel if we live today as though yesterday might reappear. This was the case for Mary, twenty-five, who had some sexual interactions with her half-brother when she was five and he was ten. Now she won't leave her kids with anybody, even at their friend's home with parents present. She uses "molesting" terms for every display of physical affection and she has cut down on sexual interest and frequency, all in an attempt to wall herself off from the feelings of shame and hurt. These desperate attempts at self-protection are not working. They only magnify her pain because they become the focus of every current moment.

I recommended serious counseling for her to get past thinking of herself as a helpless victim, now always vigilant, to an empowered, non-weak woman, now only appropriately cautious.

Paradoxically, since the past is not a current threat, some people stay there because it seems easier than handling the uncertainties of today.

Erick, thirty-nine, just found out he was adopted. He wanted to know how to deal with his feelings but couldn't quite clarify what they were. We discovered that he was wishing for another life, for other possibilities for happiness, which may, he dreamed, come to him through these new parents. Maybe he would discover something about himself or these new bio-parents that would give him something to make his life instantly easier, more happy?

I suggested that he remember that his adult life is what he created. If he were looking to these bio-parents as the genie in the bottle, he would not only be disappointed but also end up back at the beginning: with himself.

I DISRESPECT MYSELF BEFORE YOU CAN!

And this brings me to the crux of the feelings issue. When I ask callers about choices, decisions, and behaviors, which have clearly gotten them into trouble, I too often hear back, "Well, I guess I did that because I have low self-esteem." Yikes!

Chicken or the egg? Do you have to have self-esteem before or after you behave with honor and courage? Popular psychology says self-esteem comes first. So my next question becomes, "Then where the heck do you get the self-esteem?"

Harold W. Stevenson, professor of psychology at the University of Michigan, wrote in the *New York Times*: "Self-esteem theorists have it backward. Meaningful self-evaluation and positive self-esteem are usually results, not antecedents, of accomplishment. Praise is only one source of feedback; self-esteem more often comes from an awareness that the requirements of a sought-after goal have been mastered. . . . Feeling good is fine; it is even better when we have something to feel good about."

I couldn't agree more wholeheartedly. Yet low self-esteem has become one of the more revered excuses for bad choices or bad behaviors.

Incredible numbers of folks call me about not taking action in situations that called for ethics and/or guts and give as their excuse for not acting, "I guess it's because I have low self-esteem." I've asked, "Where do you think you get self-esteem from?" They answer, ". . . I dunno."

Bryan, twenty-four, felt he had no self-esteem because "my parents never told me they didn't love me, but they never told me they did, so I have a hard time loving myself. What can I do?"

When I asked Bryan what he respected in himself, he admitted that he thought himself intelligent and attractive. I told him that was good, but not all that impressive because those attributes were due to a lucky throw of the genetic dice, not the result of any action he'd taken.

"Bryan, if someone brought you a whole bucket of gold coins and dumped them in front of you, you'd feel like going shopping. But, if you'd made the effort to earn them or create them, you'd feel self-esteem."

"I hear you."

"Since you didn't earn your natural assets, they don't automatically boost your self-esteem. But if you use your intelligence creatively and generously on a difficult and risky project, now that's a different matter. So, what have you done with your potential and abilities that you admire about yourself?"

"Ummm, nothing, I think."

"Okay, Bryan, here it is. Whether or not your parents stroked you is secondary. Know why? Because supplying positive feedback regardless of the quality or reality of accomplishment is meaningless. It is what you do that ultimately determines your evaluation and respect for yourself—like taking uncomfortable risks and stretching yourself and persevering through difficult challenges."

"Oh, okay. I'm starting to understand that."

"If self-esteem is totally predicated on our parents' praise, we're all doomed if we don't get just the right words at just the right times in just the right way. It's nice if you get all that, but it isn't necessary to our well-being and success in life."

"So I have to show myself what I'm made of."

"If not, Bryan, you're just going to sit there and wonder when you're going to feel better and you're going to pick lesser types to 'hang with' rather than aspire to greater heights."

Hence, this book and my radio program are not about helping anyone feel less hurt in the moment, but to give you the tools to get better. To summarize: "Feelings, nothing but feelings . . ." obviously gets you in trouble. It's when you blend feelings with a major dose of courage, conscience, and rational thought that you connect to the most self-respectful aspects of your humanity.

5

❦

Of Course I Have Values . . . Umm, What Are They Again?
(Where Are Your Morals?)

Dr. Laura:
I would like to say I always enjoy your
program, but too often you make me look inside
myself at a a level that is not always enjoyable.
However, the results have been that I am a more
confident person because I am sure of my value,
because I am sure of my VALUES.

JoAnn

As a compass directs you through a storm at sea, values direct
you through challenges in life. Using "values" to determine your
next move is simply practical. Abdicating values to whim, immediate gratification, or voluntarily subjugating yourself to someone else's whim or gratification in order to stay "attached" gen-

erally leads to destructive behaviors. Using values is a blueprint for taking responsibility in your own life.

Here's an example of how holding her values dear would have prevented much loss and suffering for one young woman.

One of the women's magazines ran this true story as a "write in with your opinion" piece. A female dental assistant, in her early twenties, believed in virginity until marriage and considered abortion immoral. She believed, that is, until she began dating a successful male dentist in his mid to late thirties. He's reported to have "sweet-talked" her into having sex. Now, sweet talk is not rape; it is only a luscious invitation. Had she stayed firm with her virginity values . . .

She got pregnant. Evidently he told her he loved her and wanted to marry her and make a family. Someday. But not today. He suggested she have an abortion. A suggestion is not a command, it is the offering of one possible alternative. Had she stayed firm with her anti-abortion values . . .

She got an abortion. He wanted to resume their intimate sexual relationship. Perhaps she was desperate for the positive payoff (marriage) to justify in her own mind the values she had sacrificed to "keep him." She continued their sexual relationship.

She got pregnant again. He suggested abortion again. She called Mommy. Mommy called lawyer. Lawyer filed lawsuit. If the lawsuit were solely for child support, I'd applaud the action. The lover is responsible for his offspring, planned or not. But, the lawsuit went further; it attempted to make his suggestions and seductions responsible for her behavior!

Can you believe that? Here she was, a grown woman who had voluntarily abdicated her character, courage, and conscience, standing up in court and whining, "I know I went against my values, but he made me!" I get too many calls from people pleading that same pathetic excuse.

BUT . . . I'M A REBEL

Values are principles and ideas that bring meaning to the seemingly mundane experiences of life. A meaningful life that ultimately brings happiness and pride requires you to respond to temptations as well as challenges with honor, dignity, and courage. Actually, values can make difficult choices or dilemmas appear more clear-cut because they focus on concepts of ethics, virtue, and morality—qualities more resilient against "circumstance" than emotions generally turn out to be. Values ought never be the first thing you drop when you think you got a "better offer," like a rich boyfriend, or a better job with more money, or whatever your needy/greedy heart desires.

Matthew, twenty-six, the self-admitted product of a loving and together family, has been there and back:

> When I was sixteen years old—I am now twenty-five—I figured I already knew everything there was to know about the universe. In rebellion, I strove to live a life that was an exact opposite of the values I had been taught. I've done OK: no illegitimate kids, no permanent brain damage, etcetera, but in a lot of ways I've let myself down, and have always brushed off my feelings of guilt as if they were unimportant.
>
> I never realized that because of my behavior, my soul was empty. As you so aptly put it, the nobility in being a responsible adult was never there. My actions

have not been the kind to earn me the respect that my parents have been earning for themselves for over fifty years.

I started listening to your show last fall, and now have a constant reminder of the pitfalls of not thinking about my own actions. For three hours every day I listen to your opinions and find myself saying, "Yes. That is the kind of person I want to be. That is how I want to see myself, and be seen by others."

It will take a long time for my actions to outshine my dubious past, but your words have been staying with me. Over the last four to five months they have prevented me from perpetuating the kind of behavior that was self-serving and had little to do with personal responsibility. I even quote you anonymously among my peers now, and more often than not hear them say, "Yeah, I guess I just never thought about it that way." I hope that my change, over time, will lead to me re-earning the pride and respect my parents once had for me.

Thank you,
Matthew

Many young people like Matthew try to form an identity simply by going against everything they've been taught. I say "simply," because rebellion is a quick and dirty technique for standing out, as opposed to working hard at becoming someone special. It isn't really about becoming unique by efforts and commitment; it's about using the statement "everyone else is full of it" to define yourself. Pathetic and terminal, yes. Yet most, like Matthew, eventually realize their specialness evolves over time and doesn't form from the negative big bang of blind rebellion.

BUT . . . CAN'T A GROWN-UP DO WHATEVER THEY WANT?

It is during the transition to adulthood that people most often attempt to try out life without the constraints of the seemingly oppressive rules of their families, churches/temples, and society. One interesting variation on this theme is putting values into suspended animation, so you can resurrect them later. This sounds just like Zack.

Zack, twenty, is a member of a Christian church. More accurately, he was until early last year. He's bowed out for a time so that he can guiltlessly drink and have sex with his girlfriend of two years. His plan is working somewhat; he's drinking and having sex, but he isn't completely able to deaden the guilt. Darn.

By the way, he doesn't plan to marry this girl . . . because she isn't Christian "like he is." Somewhere down the road, he'll have a Christian wife and lead a Christian life, but until then . . .

I asked Zack, "Why do you think your church has these rules about premarital sex?"

He struggled with an analysis, not out of ignorance, but discomfort at looking too closely at some uncomfortable truths. "Well," he offered, "it's so you don't have babies out of wedlock and because it makes sex something special."

"If you followed your church's teachings, what would you give up?"

"I'd have to give up my girlfriend because I don't think she'd stay with me without the sex. I'd have to give up the sex and I like it."

"Okay, Zack, to keep her and to enjoy sex you have to pay a price. What is that?"

"Well, I feel uncomfortable about it all. I miss some

things about the church, but I'll get back to it someday."

"Bottom line, Zack, is that the drinking and the sex are pleasurable right now. But, all in all, you're not too happy?"

Silence.

Bummer! Can't have happiness and pleasure all at the same time? Yes you can! It's just that "timing" and "context" are important. Just because you're at the water, do you have to swim? What if you don't know how yet and it's shark season and the water is polluted and the powerboats are racing about and a hurricane is coming in . . . then what? Likewise, wine with dinner can be a good thing. Getting sloshed to have "fun," to get your conscience and good sense out of the way, or to hide from problems is not a good thing. The "rules," the "values," are to help you develop character; that is, the ability to deal courageously with moments that promise pleasure at the same time they practically guarantee problems.

VALUES VACCINATE AGAINST FUTURE PAIN

Noelle, twenty-one, wrote a letter to the editor of the *Valley Press/Antelope Valley* in response to the question, Reasons to Stay Chaste:

> I am twenty-one years old, and I am a virgin. I plan to stay that way until I get married. Let me tell you the reasons I made this choice.
>
> The most obvious reasons are health-related. I don't want to get pregnant or catch any disease. There is protection out there to provide safer sex, but it isn't infallible. Why take a chance, however small, especially with a disease like AIDS? Yes, some STDs are curable, but some are not. Complications

can result, such as pelvic inflammatory disease, which may lead to infertility or tubal pregnancies.

I have chosen abstinence also because of friends' relationships damaged by having sex without commitment and trust that only marriage provides. Some have suffered terribly because sex made them feel so close and bonded to someone only to later realize that it wasn't the right person after all; they had given themselves so entirely to the other person that they felt they had lost part of themselves when they broke up.

Others have had sex so often and with so many people that it means nothing to them; I wonder how such an intimate act can be considered nothing special.

Noelle expresses a sentiment that is sadly neglected in this "do whatever you want" era: Values not only make sense, they literally save people unnecessary pain! We don't hear nearly enough about the "practicality" of ethical behavior. When I ask callers why they follow the rules learned from their parents or religion, I rarely get back the "pragmatic intent" of the rule, just that they were taught the rule. Perhaps it is in teaching these rules without stressing practicality along with spirituality that some families and religious disciplines go wrong.

DOING GOOD BECOMES ITS OWN REWARD

To the many people who are struggling with the tugs-of-war between pleasure now and happiness later, I always remind how indeed a deep happiness rarely comes from immediately pleasurable behaviors and experiences. Pleasure is time-limited to the pleasurable input. When the input ends, the awareness of pleasure fades fast. Happiness, on the other hand, does not require the continuous input of anything. It is fueled by its own appreciation.

A woman came up to me at a book signing and said with great pride and abundant smiles, "I gave up a man because he really needed to be with his children and he couldn't do that in a relationship with me in a different city. So, I gave him up, and while I miss him terribly, I am happy every day about the good thing I did. I got that from listening to you, Dr. Laura. Thank you."

Pleasure would be reveling in his arms each night. Happiness is letting him go in order to do the "right thing." This is the perspective that must be taught, reinforced, and celebrated.

WHEW! CLOSE CALL

Chris, twenty-one, phoned my program all upset. He had planned to stay a virgin until marriage, but . . . the other night he had unprotected sex with a girl he hardly knows. It scared him to realize that he risked his health and life on a "quickie"!

"Dr. Laura, I hope you're going to be tough with me, I need it. I'm not a stupid person, I know the risks. It is scaring me. I'm debating how I should take responsibility for it. I might have gotten a disease, maybe not."

"Chris, let's assume for a moment that you got lucky and nothing 'biological' is going to happen. Are you so shallow that this action has no psychological, emotional, philosophical, or spiritual impact? You did tell me to be tough with you!"

"That's a good question."

"So if you don't get a sexually transmitted disease, we're

covered? You are a human being. The sex act had no profound meaning past 'Ohhh, baby, don't stop now,' or something you could have done yourself? The act is the act. The meaning behind our acts is what gives us meaning as individuals and as a society. Doesn't 'just doin' it' take something away from it for you?"

"Well, it does. Obviously this was a very shallow act and one with no important emotions attached to it. And I'm thinking that I'm worth more than that. I think that I want to remain celibate until I'm in a serious, loving, committed relationship. It doesn't have to be marriage, but it would certainly be one with caring and love and monogamy. Otherwise, it is shallow."

ABRACADABRA—VALUES, DO YOUR STUFF!

Stephanie, twenty-one, is a virgin and had planned to stay that way until she's married. But now she finds herself very attracted to somebody . . . did I say "very"? She'd hoped that her values, the rules, would protect her from temptation. Now she is set adrift without a paddle because she discovered that values don't function like an automatic, invisible protective shield.

"Just in case I start dating him, do you have any advice on how to stay a virgin?"

"You mean you have values until temptations ride into town, then the values sneak out during the night? The town ain't big enough for both values and temptations. Values keep us steady through times of deep temptation. They are our road map through the minefields of challenge. It is easy to say you have values, and easier still to live up to them when you're by yourself in the middle of the ocean."

"That's true."

"Values are truly only shown to exist when they are tested. If it is meaningful for you to reserve sexual intimacy for marital vows, if you feel that doing so elevates sex and you, that is admirable."

"Yeah, but how do you make the values do their thing to keep you from doing something else?"

"Values only have the power you infuse into them with your respect for them and yourself, and your will. Values without temptations are merely lofty ideas. Expediting them is what makes you, and them, special. That requires grit, will, sacrifice, courage, and discomfort. But it is in the difficulty that both the values and you gain importance. The measure of you as a human being is how you honor the values.

"When you begin dating him, clarify your position of intercourse only within marriage. If he tries to push you away from that position, you know he values you only as a means to sexual gratification. If he gets seductive and you're lubricating from your eyeballs to your ankles, this is the moment when you choose between momentary pleasure and long-term self-respect."

"That is the real choice I'm making at that point, isn't it."

There is no fast lane to self-esteem. It's won on these battlegrounds where immediate gratification comes up against character. When character triumphs, self-esteem heightens.

One caller asked, "What if I'm too weak?" I answered that the road to unhappiness and low self-esteem is paved with the victories of immediate gratification.

SURE I'M COMMITTED . . . OOPS . . . BYE-BYE

Simply saying words such as *committed* or *love* does not mean there actually is commitment or love. Then why say the words? Because of the instant gratification brought upon by such declarations; gratifications like sex or enhanced (temporary, of course) sense of self. Listen to Cliff:

Cliff, thirty-nine, is in a difficult situation right now. He's been dating a twenty-seven-year-old woman for two and a half months. That's ten weeks of weekends they spent together, amounting to about twenty days of actual contact time.

"We had a committed relationship and it seemed like our relationship was made in heaven. Then she was diagnosed with lupus and I went over to talk with her and tried to explain my feelings."

"What feelings are those, Cliff?"

"That I can't marry her because of her health condition."

"I guess you only enjoy relationships when they look like they're made in heaven, and don't come burdened with the realities of earth."

"Well, I suppose. Maybe 'made in heaven' was a poor choice of words."

"No, I imagine it accurately expresses that you like your relationship pretty and neat."

"Well, yeah."

"Cliff, I don't know if you're ever going to find a perfect situation with nothing unpleasant or challenging to deal with, but I guess you could just move on and keep trying."

"If we were already married, it would be a life-long commitment and that would be different."

"You already used the word *committed* before. You said you were committed already."

"I didn't mean that really."

"I guess you really meant the sex was good and she was fun."

"Is there a way to explain my feelings to her?"

"Are you looking for her to give you permission to abandon her? Are you looking for forgiveness for jumping ship? Then Cliff, just say good-bye. Let her get on with what she has to deal with, with the people who will stand by her."

"That's pretty much what I was looking at myself. Maybe I shouldn't try to drag it out."

"It's painful enough for her to have to deal with this lupus diagnosis without having the person who has been 'committed,' whom she's been bedding for two and a half months, pull back self-protectively. This just adds to the self-loathing people often have to go through in the beginning of coping with an illness. It just adds to her pain."

"Maybe I sound like a terrible person."

"Cliff, you're not winning a lot of points with me. Your knee-jerk reaction is to withdraw. That's to take care of you. You're not even reserving judgment to see what evolves. Realistically, there isn't much between you. Your predicament shows why infatuation and recreational sex should not be used as criteria for the notion of commitment. You are at the point of committed to good sex, good times, good fun, good feelings."

Cliff had sex, which I think ought to be serious business, and told his lady he was committed; when there was an opportunity to show that the commitment meant something, he showed it meant nothing. That is the measure of Cliff as a person, and that is the Cliff he takes with him when he leaves the relationship.

Now, don't think for a moment I'm placing all the blame on Cliff and making the lady a total victim. I'm holding Cliff accountable for his charade about so-called committed words and behaviors. I always hold everyone, women and men, accountable for their cooperation, enjoyment, and participation in such charades. Considering the difference in male and female emotionality and biology, women usually pay the bigger price. Sadly, what follows proves that point.

Tracey, twenty-six, had a problem: "I'm pregnant. I'm living with my boyfriend of almost a year now and I'm really terrified about what is going on here. There is no trust in the relationship and I don't know what to do."

"Terrified? Of some danger?"

"No, no, no. I have a dependency about needing people. I just wanted some advice on how I should handle dealing with this. We're not staying together and we made a baby."

"You may want to consider adoption of the baby to an intact, stable, non-terrified, two-parent family. Maybe that's the best thing you could do for the child while you're trying to straighten out your life. There is no greater love than that kind of sacrifice, probably because it is so unself-centered."

(Tracey is crying). "Wow. Okay. It's a hard decision."

"That's right. Tracey, one of the steps away from being your self-described dependent frightened type is to take on a situation like this with the courage to tap the stronger parts of you, and do the right thing by this baby. When you look at the alternative of single motherhood, it too often means being a non-mother because you have to work to pay the bills and the child is brought up by an institutionalized day-care situation. No research indicates full-time day care is better for children than families, unless of course it's the Manson family. Also, one way or another, you'll have to deal for life with the bio-dad, with whom there wasn't a plan to make a baby, nor interest in being a dad. The legal and emotional issues are significant here."

Cliff with his "perfect little relationship" came up against an oopsie when his perfect lady got ill. Tracey with her "I need you 'cause without you there's no me" came up against an oopsie when she got pregnant and the guy showed he wasn't playing for keeps. Both Cliff and Tracey toyed with commitment, sex, and togetherness instead of choosing the tougher, uphill, sometimes bumpy road toward meaningful intimacy.

Whenever choices are made morality is immediately an issue. A lion kills a baby antelope because it is driven by instinct to do so. There is no choice involved, therefore there is no right and wrong about the deed. However, when human beings act it is always a moral issue: right or wrong, noble or cowardly, compassionate or selfish. Tracey and Cliff wanted to feel "real good" and they wanted it "right now." Now, in both cases, others are hurt or threatened.

Some people actually don't much care about that.

BUT . . . I'M GETTIN' MINE!

Anthony, twenty-four, really got my attention. His lady friend is twenty-five, divorced, with three little girls, five, four, and two.

"Anthony, with three little kids, why did they divorce?"

"Well, we had an affair and made a baby."

"Then, there are four children?"

"Yes, she is fourteen months old. Now the conflict is that we want to be together and maybe get married someday, but I show a lot of favoritism to my daughter. I have negative feelings toward the other girls."

"You contributed to the destruction of their family. You owe it to them to at least be kind. You really wanted to pluck her out of the situation and leave the kids behind, I bet."

"I don't feel I have much control over myself."

"You can choose not to exert control. You can choose to exert control. Basically, you're selfish and don't want to bother with what isn't 'yours.'"

"Yeah, that's right. And it's messing up our goal of being a family."

Frankly, friends, that's where I lost it. This woman has three babies under five and is screwing around on her husband, unprotected sex gets her pregnant, she moves far away from the children's dad, thereby limiting their access to their dad. This guy helps her to do all of this and he is now showing some weak concern about "family values"? Oh puhleese.

And, just when you think it can't get worse . . .

BUT . . . IT WAS A "BEST LAID PLAN"

Karen and Lee wanted me to take sides in the issue of where their planned-for child should live. Don't let the "planned-for" get your hopes up. This situation is horrendous.

Karen and Lee are the parents of an eighteen-month-old boy. They are not married. They do not live together. And, they actually planned it all this way!

"You mean that this kid is not an oopsie?"

"Oh, no!" replied Karen.

"You guys actually said to each other that you didn't want to marry each other, but let's make a kid? Kids basically like and benefit from a mom and dad under the same roof. You don't care for each other enough to get married. Don't you realize you're together forever anyway through this child?"

"Yeah, that's basically it. When we were together we had another child and lost it through a terminal illness. We then knew we didn't want to be together but we were broken-hearted over our first child's death so we wanted to have another one. We made a commitment to this child even though we couldn't make one to each other."

"What happens when one or both of you gets married to someone else?"

"Well, we both already are in relationships. We discussed

all about living in the same city no matter what. Even though we're not married we still think we can be great parents."

"Would you recommend this scheme to your boy when he grows up and is ready to mate or parent?"

"No, I wouldn't."

"Why?"

"This is a selfish move I know."

"Thank you for admitting to that. It is certainly not the best plan for a kid."

"I agree."

Lee chimed in here. "We're both real happy with the baby but our situation is that we've changed the visitation. Up until two weeks ago I would have the kid two days a week for ten hours. And what we have done is have me take him overnight. It didn't work out, he cried all night. He was up all night. It got a little better after that."

"That's not unusual behavior for kids to wake up and cry; there are lots of sleep problems in his age range."

Karen asked, "Well, do you think at his age he should be sleeping in his dad's house or still only sleep at my house?"

"See," I said to them both, "this is one of the reasons you don't make babies under these conditions, because you have to ask these sorts of questions. And a turf war is beginning between the two of you."

"I know, but . . ." replied Karen.

"Yeah, I know, but I wanna do what I wanna do," I interrupted.

"We're going to do whatever is best for him," Karen said.

"Working on your relationship and getting married would be the best for him." Karen laughed. "If you two can get along well enough to have intercourse enough times to make him, and get along well enough to team up for this scheme, I don't understand what you can't work through in order to get married and be a family for the boy. The boy needs a single nest; not to be visiting two turfs and not have one place of his own to call home."

Karen shot back with, "He has a nest here with me."

"Then, perhaps he should always be there and bio-dad comes and visits child who is on his own turf. Your boy is not a pet or a piece of furniture you two can share at whim. He is a human being and his rights and needs have never been put first. So, if he stays with you, Karen, Dad should come over every day and play, feed, wash, and put him to bed."

"No, not every day," Karen complained quickly.

"Yes, Karen, every day. That's what a boy needs from his dad every day. I don't much care how inconvenient it is for you. You made this human being voluntarily to replace the child you lost. You two were only thinking of yourselves. You weren't thinking of the child or the ramifications.

"Lee, you should be with your boy every day. And when you get married and have four other kids, you'll have to figure out a way to be with this boy and your four kids and your wife simultaneously every day.

"All this will limit both of you in your dealings with your new dearly beloveds, who might not be as interested in this time-sharing technique of parenting as you are. Karen, you need to marry a guy who understands that Lee will be there every day. And Lee, you need to tell any future mate that for a certain portion of every day you will be at Karen's house parenting your child.

"I'm only helping to reinforce what you folks said you wanted to do, and that was whatever was best for the child. This child needs both parents every day."

Frankly, I am horrified at what Karen and Lee did. They intended to condemn this child, even before birth, to a broken home. This is not an acceptable alternative family life-style. It is a tragedy for the child.

Discussing this moral crisis of just such creative "family constructs" Rabbi Jonathan Sacks wrote in *The Ottowa Citizen,* March 31, 1995:

> Unquestionably, though, the greatest victims have been children themselves. In the field of personal relationships, two systems of thought, two ways of life, have collided, one which speaks of interdependence, the other of independence. The battle against the family has been conducted in terms of rights—the rights of men to have relationships unemcumbered by lasting duties, the rights of women to be free of men, the rights of each of us to plot our private paths to happiness, undistracted by the claims of others. . . . What remains are fragments, temporary attachments, terminable and contractual arrangements, unpredictable sequences in which our lives are thrown together without expectation, hope, or emotional investment.

There it is, the collision between personal, immediate gratification ("Don't I deserve to be happy?) and the needs of others, especially children. Many people talk a good game about caring to do the right thing . . . that is, until . . .

BUT . . . I GOT A BETTER OFFER

Mike, thirty-eight, divorced after twelve years of marriage with two children, ten and eleven, is confused. The dilemma is how you choose between his kids' needs and his own immediate happiness.

His new lady, twenty-eight, gets "pissed off" if he sees his kids a lot. It seems that she was abandoned by her dad when she was little. Now she is hell-bent to make sure that no matter how many actual children are abandoned on her watch, that she won't ever be abandoned again. You see, friends, I consider her actions evil. She is intentionally hurting others for self-gain, -gratification, and -satisfaction. By the way, said girlfriend has a one-year-old child from some guy who is out of the picture. Oh yes, she orchestrated her own child's abandonment.

Even more sickening is Mike's weakness in the face of this evil. He's actually feeling like a "saint" for saving her from all the pain in her life—while looking for a way to make his own life less tumultuous. Mike is actually considering abandoning his kids to make his own life more serene. He knows it isn't the right thing to do . . . but I guess he feels that life with her is a "better offer."

How in the world can giving up values to reduce conflict make anyone truly happy?

From Leo Rosten come these words: "I cannot believe that the purpose of life is to be 'happy.' I think the purpose of life is to be useful, to be responsible, to be compassionate. It is above all, to matter, to count, to stand for something, to have made some difference that you lived at all."

And as Tish wrote:

> I am currently reading your book *Ten Stupid Things Women Do to Mess Up Their Lives* and am realizing how much of this I already knew but didn't find the strength to change or help myself. I need to stick to my values and quit making the same stupid mistakes and stupid choices. You're right about women bringing things on themselves. That's fact. I want to be more confident, mature, and secure, and I know only I can made that happen.

Happiness, therefore, is about "mattering," and mattering is about valuing things and living accordingly. Trying to bypass that truth usually means you give up your values for a short-term thrill: a false sense of security or belonging, as remedy for loneliness or in a distorted attempt to seem all together.

BUT . . . I HAVE PSYCHOLOGICAL PROBLEMS

Too much inappropriate behavior is done in the name of "psychological problems." This is where therapists often miss an opportunity to deal with the potentially self-/other-destructive behaviors generated by their clients' attempts to belatedly and inappropriately deal with childhood pain, trauma, or confusions. A good example of what I mean is described in this letter from Cindy:

> I am twenty-six, single, never married, good job, hard worker. I have for the past two years dated and slept with men I thought I liked and would settle for later to realize that I was lonely and bored and not being selective. I think my problem for the last two years has been wanting to be in "a relationship" and not paying much attention to who it is with. My parents are divorced (I'm a firm believer that most things relate to childhood) and I don't have too much of a father figure except for a godfather who was great in being a nice, honest, and very decent person but was a little reserved with children. So, I believe that I seek the loving, nurturing father figure in a man, yet I have this crazy desire to pulverize each guy that comes along and destroy the relationship before it has the chance to get started. I think

maybe I do it to protect myself and not get hurt and keep safely distant. Do I make sense?

Not only does Cindy make sense, she has a profound understanding of the motivating dynamics behind her behaviors. She knows that she's missing "father love" and yearns for it. At the same time, she is angry about past loss and angry about potential loss with a new guy. Hence she has sex (the closeness) and then blows them out of the water (revenge and self-protection). This insight is magnificent, but not enough!

It is at this point that a therapist would serve Cindy well by having her bypass the destructive behaviors by putting the issue of values in front of her: for example, using people sexually for immediate intimacy gratification, punishing individual men for the pain she experienced with the loss of Dad, doing hurtful behaviors toward these men to keep the "upper hand" and be able to justify the inevitable rejection.

Pain and fears are not licenses to hurt others. All of Cindy's actions may be understandable psychological constructs, but they are "in principle" not moral behaviors. She needs to know that her hurt and self-protective concerns have driven her to become "the enemy." She needs to be held accountable for these actions in spite of her historical losses. True freedom from the self-imposed tyranny of the past will be to use courage to get her important, and very human, needs met in healthier, more creative ways.

One argument against my position would be that telling her this would demoralize her and lower her self-esteem; she requires compassion, after all, she's been hurt—isn't this like kicking someone when they're down? No, quite the opposite. Her self-esteem and demoralization already exist and are being continually massaged by her destructive behaviors! My position is that by acknowledging the "wrongness" of her current actions she gives herself a concrete way out of misery.

My experience on-air with these situations generally ends on a positive note. I tell callers that the first thing they have to do is to stop hurting and using others. Believe it or not, their first reaction is usually one of surprise because in their "my feelings" mode they hadn't considered the pain they were bringing to others. Nor had they thought much about the self-indulgent nature of their actions. Redirecting their attention outward is already a benevolent and life-affirming change.

As I mentioned before, therapists might benefit their client's growth by introducing "principles," i.e., values and basic morals (issues of right and wrong actions), into the therapeutic process. It is more humanizing to hold individuals accountable for the hurt they cause than to forgive them their continuing transgressions because they "hurt," or to postpone changing actions until they really understand their historical pain. The former indicates the therapist's recognition of their adultness and strength. The latter agrees with the weakest and worst part of their being. And practically speaking, people don't "move" until the pain gets too great. Eliminating the opportunity to diminish the pain through these other behaviors increases the pain, thereby increasing the motivation to change.

What makes people truly human is the recognition and contemplation of the morality made at each moment. Crickets make noise because they biologically have to. Therapists should always help the individual hold on to their "humanness" by bringing up the importance of courage and conscience in making moment-to-moment principled decisions, regardless of their fears.

Having "dealt" with a problem or issue does not mean the

matter is erased; it simply means that the individual can behave appropriately in spite of the problems or issues. Isn't that the greatest lesson of perspective?

Yet perspective, especially moral perspective, is abdicated all the time for all sorts of me-me-me motivations, such as . . .

BUT . . . HE MADE ME FEEL GOOD

Laurie, thirty, has been married seven months to a thirty-seven-year-old man who has three daughters, thirteen, fifteen, seventeen . . . and a one-year-old son.

"Wait a minute, Laurie. You've been married seven months and a one-year-old is your stepson? He made this baby, dumped his wife, and went off with you?"

"Well, she wasn't his wife, she was kind of a fling."

"You mean he fooled around on both his wife and you?"

"We were just friends then. We started dating when she was about six months pregnant."

"You knew you were dating a guy who had just got some-one pregnant?"

"Well, he didn't want it and he wasn't careful, I guess," Laurie said, laughing. "But, that's not the reason I'm calling."

"Why not? Is he paying child support and seeing the infant?"

"He sees the boy during lunchtime maybe twice a week. Soon he can have him for overnight visits."

"I think it's sad that men like him get rewarded with yet another woman." (Laurie laughs again). "Did that make you laugh?"

"I don't know."

"He was in the process of divorcing his wife and leaving his three kids, makes another with another woman, then starts dating you. What would you tell your daughter about dating a guy with this track record?"

"I don't know, I guess I would say she's a fool."

"And why would you think her a fool?"

"Knowing the situation I'd think he just doesn't take responsibility for what he is doing."

"How were you able to rationalize all this away?"

"I don't know if I have."

"You had to say to yourself at some point that you know another woman is pregnant with his baby and he's dating me, but that's okay because . . . "

"Because he said things that made me feel good."

"And the most important thing is that 'I feel good' right now. Too many women have so little sense of values and so little sense, period, that they hook up to a guy who they know probably isn't there for the long haul."

"Yeah, I have two kids from my previous marriage, three and five. His thirteen-year-old comes over every other week and doesn't want to have anything to do with me or my boys. She just wants her dad alone. So, they take off by themselves."

"Sounds right to me."

"The whole weekend?"

"She only gets him four days a month!"

"That's what he said."

"That's the price you have to pay for hooking up with a guy who makes babies in a number of places."

"Shouldn't attempts be made to be a family?"

"She had a family. Now she's got competition for fragments of her father's attention and love divided under three roofs. How do you think you'd feel? This situation is a reality of repetitive marriages and/or baby-making. I can't make it go away. You built this house with a lot of broken parts and you're mad 'cause it doesn't look perfect. You can't force kids to love and be attached. You have to make the best of things, realizing you will never get his full attention and energies."

Laurie didn't want to anticipate the realities and complexities because this man "made her feel good." Here's a guy who has made four children with two women and he hasn't stayed put in either place. She's divorced with two little children and he seems like a good bet for future security? I don't think so.

Some women are driven even further to clear the playing field of debris like old wives and former children.

BUT . . . IT'S JUST A SMALL REWRITE OF HISTORY

Rosemary, fifty-two, is complaining about her husband's ex-wife. He had three children with the ex-wife in their sixteen years of marriage. The children are fourteen, eleven, and six. And he left six years ago. You do the math.

This guy made a kid with his wife and immediately walked out? I imagine any wife (or ex) would be bitchy about that. I asked Rosemary why she took him after he had just abandoned three kids. Her answer was, "He did?" I asked her what she'd call it and she explained that it was the wife who had wanted the third child. "So, he went to bed with her and had several unprotected sexual experiences to make sure that wouldn't happen?" I challenged.

It amazes me how Rosemary wanted to make the ex responsible. If he didn't want more children and was clear about wanting to leave the marriage, he could have used contraceptives, not had sex, or gotten sterilized.

"Rosemary, for the life of me I don't understand why women want men who have abandoned their babies."

"He really didn't want to have more kids."

"Then he could have kept his penis in his pants. He's playing victim, and you're backing him up!"

"My question is about her telling the children he abandoned them. I don't think she should be doing that."

"But, Rosemary, he did! You just don't want to face the truth. He did what he wanted sexually and then left her with the consequences. What you call a husband, I call a creep. I don't think it's good for the children for her to constantly tell them that their father abandoned them, but I'm here to tell you that this was precisely what he did. If he hadn't left, she wouldn't have that as truth to say!"

"Okay."

"Does he help them with their homework every day?"

"No, they live in Baltimore, and we're in L.A. She wanted to move closer to her family, and they both agreed to it."

"If he were on the phone with me now, I'd tell him to move to Baltimore and parent his kids."

"Really?"

"Leaving them and then letting them go far away is double abandonment. Ultimately, he didn't care to be in their lives every day. And he found a nice woman like you to take him in. I just don't understand it."

Actually, I do understand it. It comes down to getting needs met at almost any cost, and then finding some way (as though it was only the ex-wife who got pregnant by herself and he was only being nice in letting her move 2,000 miles away with his children) to make it seem okay.

Suzanne, twenty-seven, called, I think, to have me cut her off at the pass, she knew the way she was getting her needs met might cost her too much.

BUT . . . I WANT TO RECONSTITUTE
LOST FEELINGS

Suzanne's relationship of two years ended one and a half months ago. She had counted on this relationship to go the distance. She called because "I know how I was brought up . . . but I'm questioning the rules about sex and intimacy. I mean, why not just go out and do it."

Suzanne had never been sexually intimate with her now ex, and she was stinging from the rejection and missing the closeness. Her anger at the loss when doing things the "right way" made her doubt both the meaningfulness and usefulness of that "right way." She's just gonna have fun now, and the hell with the values.

When we can't get back at the person who caused us the pain, or we realize we don't really have just cause to punish them (people are entitled to their choices), we sometimes turn that anger (it's really pain) inward. And "going to hell with yourself" by drinking, smoking, and "doing it" are often the tactics chosen.

I reminded Suzanne that losing this man was one thing, losing the hopes, sense of attachment, and closeness another, but that losing oneself by abdicating one's values was the worst loss of all.

BUT . . . TOO PIOUS, TOO LATE

Jovanna, twenty, is from Peru and has been in the U.S.A. for five years. She is also five months pregnant and not married. The "father" is her boyfriend, who is an Orthodox Russian Jew. She is Catholic. He won't marry her or even bring her home to his family because she is a non-Jew. She is in pain.

Yes, both her religion and his speak of no premarital sexual intimacies . . . but it felt so good. Now she understands one of the serious cornerstones of that ubiquitous rule. He wants her to get an abortion or just go away, or both.

I suggested she go to an attorney and get the proper forms so bio-dad can sign away his parental rights so that she could put the child up for adoption by a two-parent family. I suggested further that she deliver the form to his home (where he lives with his parents) dressed in maternity clothes and smiling sweetly at his parents.

She hesitated because she worried about his getting "mad at her." Can you believe that?

In addition to the "feeling good" type of motivation for abdicating values, there is the other powerful force: expediency.

BUT . . . IT IS EXPEDIENT

Pam, thirty-two, is dealing with infertility issues. Thanks to biotechnology she has an answer: in-vitro fertilization, where she will be implanted with four to five fertilized eggs. The doctor explained to her that the procedure could produce too many embryos. Therefore, to insure one "good one," they would go in and selectively terminate all but one embryo.

She was calling me because she was uneasy about this "selection and termination process." Pam was desperate to finally have a child. After years of emotional pain and expensive medical tests and procedures, this was her last hope.

What a terrible irony: here is a woman hoping to create a life, and the road to that life will be paved with deaths.

I suggested that she was so focused on the result (child), she was perhaps too willing to justify the means (selective abortions). She tearfully agreed. We spoke of alternatives, from using only eggs to be fertilized and implanted (and deal with the "fraternal twin" possibility) to adoption. Both of those alternatives had limitations. Using less eggs meant more of the expensive procedures before "statistical probability" rewarded her, and adoption meant more waiting and missing the physical experience of pregnancy.

However, Pam did agree that those alternatives, while having hefty price tags, did not leave her with the intentional destruction of life. All during our conversation Pam had been bemoaning that her desire for a baby was costing her her values. Ultimately, she decided the cost was too high and that she would tell the doctor that the selective terminations were not an option.

BUT . . . IT SOUNDS GOOD

Honor only becomes relevant where there is challenge to the character. Otherwise, anyone can sound "good." A major part of honor is personal responsibility versus situational advantages. One particular news item in 1994 highlighted this issue. A forty-year-old woman was jogging alone in a state park when she was killed by a mountain lion. Almost immediately, a lawyer was involved in a suit against the state, because of the state's failure to manage the mountain lion population and because it didn't react to reports of cougar activity in the area by posting warning signs. However, some time later, the woman's husband decided to drop his $10,000 claim, stating, "Barbara and I have always taken responsibility for our own actions. Barbara chose to run in the wilds and, on a very long shot, did not come back. This is not really the fault of the state. In my opinion, people should take responsibility for themselves."

When painful and difficult events occur, people are highly

motivated to "find fault." Part of the reason is our need to understand the cause and effect of a situation, to relieve anxiety about our ultimate, and feared, vulnerability (what we know we can fight). Another aspect is defensiveness about being the bad boy/girl, since assigning external blame gets us off the hook. A third facet of finding fault is dealing with our "pain and fear" by turning into righteous anger.

Too often our defensiveness about possibly being the bad boy/girl gets in the way of our value judgments where and when we need them the most.

BUT . . . THEN *I'LL* BE JUDGED

For two months, Debra, forty-three, has been dating a thirty-two-year-old divorced man with two children, six and nine.

"I know more about him than he knows about me. And that's my question. I don't know how much to tell him about things of my past. I have many things I'm not proud of and don't even want to tell you."

"Debra, okay, without telling me what the things are, why did you do so many things you're not proud of? That's more important to me than the actual 'things.'"

"Well, I think part of it was I felt pressured from other people. It was adventurous. It was pleasing other people. I didn't know how to say no. I didn't have a good value system."

"These are character issues."

"Yes, I know. How much of this bad stuff should I reveal if I'm not doing it anymore? It was ten years ago."

"Debra, how is it you are not dating a peer, someone closer in age?"

"This is the first time I've had a younger fellow. He's divorced with two kids, six and nine."

"How much time does your boyfriend spend with them?"

"Not a whole lot."

"Then, why do you want him? You said earlier that you didn't have a value system ten years ago, but that you've changed. Why do you want a divorced man, with little kids, who doesn't spend a lot of time with them? I would hope that you would look at such a man and say he's unacceptable because of low character, as evidenced by his lack of investment in these minor, dependent children. I didn't ask you what your 'bad things' are . . . what's more important is what you are. And part of what you are is determined by what you value and accept in behavior from others, and not just what it is toward you."

"I agree."

"Values involve not only how you behave, but the behavior you accept in others you are intimate with. If you accept inappropriate behaviors, your value system is still wanting because you are saying, 'As long as I get mine.' "

"Yeah, well, I haven't been thinking about that at all, just about my embarrassments. My selfish part is tickled here."

"Well, Debra, think about dumping this man because he doesn't parent his kids. Then think about him calling you in six months having changed his behaviors because you made him realize something. Imagine him telling you he is impressed with the quality of you as a woman and person because you took such a stand. Frankly, if he calls or not, this is the ultimate reward for your changes in values and character."

Debra laughs. "Well, I didn't say I was perfect."

What's with this "nobody is perfect" excuse? I'm quite amused by the attempt to excuse not trying harder, by claiming that perfect is not possible; it may not be, but striving toward it as an ideal is! It is in the act of "striving" that we demonstrate character, courage, and conscience.

BUT . . . PERFECT AIN'T POSSIBLE

I have been in too many "debates" in which the terms "perfect," or "ideal," are denigrated. Denigrated! The implication being that it is ultimately unattainable therefore dispensable.

For example, during "Women's Night," a radio broadcast in which I was the only panel member with a child who was also married, the issue of child care came up. I stated that the ideal situation for a child was a two-parent family with no full-time day care and no part-time day care till the child was at least two and a half to three years old. I was treated to angry rhetoric: "Yeah, that's nice, but that's the ideal, and the ideal is not possible, and I don't want to be put down like I'm doing something bad to my kid."

It went on from there, but you get the idea. I was the living embodiment of that so-called impossible ideal, but the ideal is not possible? Millions in America are living up to the ideal, but the ideal is not possible? The real problem in that room was that the ideal was not valued. When the ideal is valued, people make the sacrifices and efforts necessary to try to reach it. Bad stuff happens, and when it does, you simply do your best with the situation. However, that is different from devaluing the ideal, never working toward it, and expecting no judgment and no negative consequences.

BUT . . . THE SHOE FITS

Judgments are absolutely necessary. Without them, the issue of choice has no meaning because everything is equal.

Tisa, thirty-five, has a five-year-old son and a four-month-old son. Her husband left when she was pregnant with the second child and has been shacking up with his new honey. As a parent, Tisa is confused about how to bridge the issue of making a judgment (Dad did something bad or wrong) and acceptance (he's your dad, he loves you).

Up to now she's tried to be truthful with her son about what Dad did, that abandoning your family is bad. But she also tells son that "Dad loves you," because she is trying to maintain the relationship between the boy and his dad. Believe it or not, the guy told her that she's poisoning the kid against him—by simply reiterating the truth. I told her to tell him for me that he's the one who has done the poisoning! He expects that there be no judgment, as though judgment were wrong but his abandonment wasn't. Unbelievable. Is the solution to give the child the impression that these actions are a normal part of marriage and family? I think not.

Frankly, it never ceases to amaze me how blind some people wish to be about their actions, as though their search for happiness and comfort precluded the right of judgment against them. Interestingly, they don't seem to give up their judging of others.

BUT . . . I'M MORE RIGHT

Janet is forty, with two children, fourteen and sixteen. She has been dating a fellow for three years, engaged for two, with no wedding date set. He has custody of his three children, nine, eleven, and thirteen. She's begun living with him and is critical of his children for being impulsive, wild, and undisciplined.

I was stunned. I asked Janet if living together without a formal marriage, without even a wedding date, didn't show her to be impulsive and undisciplined. She sure isn't role-modeling the behaviors she was demanding from his children!

Don't think for a moment that I don't believe in the moral

necessity for judging the behaviors, actions, and choices of others. You must filter what you permit into your life, what you support, and thereby allow to continue. Would you, upon deciding to adopt a dog, not observe and judge the behaviors of many dogs before deciding which would be the most appropriate in your home? Do you really want to bring home that frothing pit bull to play with your two-year-old child? When it's put that way, it all seems obvious, doesn't it?

Well, there are those who purport not to judge because the situation simply doesn't involve them personally. I recently heard one radio talk-show host debating another over the issue of getting involved in circumstances that "don't really impact you."

BUT . . . IT AIN'T HURTIN' ME

The subject was a recent furor over a judge who continued to have his child in the Boy Scouts, despite knowing that the Scouts "illegally" prohibited homosexual members and leaders. The issue was that, since the judge was part of the legal system, should he be involved in an organization that condoned illegal discriminatory practices?

The host's partner asked this question: "Would you belong to a club that disallowed Jews and blacks?" The host said, "Yes, if my wife and I liked the food and the golf course."

I was completely sickened and spoke to him personally about those remarks. He seemed oblivious to the moral issue. I explained that it was immoral to stand by and watch "wrong" being done and that this amounted to no less than passive support, but support nonetheless. He blinked, and said that he "just didn't see it that way." I tried to bring the matter closer to home by reminding him he was looking into the face of a Jew and that my producer standing four feet from him was black and that we wouldn't be allowed in. "Well," he said, and laughed, "we'd make an exception for you!" I told him that "it would be immoral for me to enjoy exceptionhood under those circumstances."

"This is just a difference of opinion," he said as he nervously left my office. "I still consider you a friend."

"This is about a difference in character," I responded. "I regret I can't reciprocate your sentiments."

When character, not opinion, is the issue, the moral obligation to stand behind "right" becomes not only the measure of you as a person, but portends the way of the world. Such judgment and response helps guide the world toward the ideal ever so asymptotically.

BUT . . . NO FAIR! I'M BEING SHUNNED

Adam, thirty, called me all upset. He's out of the air force, voluntarily unemployed, and sexually servicing a fifty-year-old married woman who takes financial care of him in return. Adam's sister, a psychiatrist in the air force and a religious person, won't talk to him.

Why was he calling? He wanted to change his sister's behavior, to get his sister to talk to him again. When I suggested that he already had the key to that, which was demonstrating pride toward honorable work, he quipped, "I'm addicted to the money," and he laughed.

Adam figured being a gigolo was easy money and not hurting anybody, so what was his sister's problem? I suggested that his sister saw the hurt that he ignored: the betrayal of the woman's husband and siphoning off of his family's financial resources, among them. His sister also valued the sanctity of sex, of marriage vows, and of pride in one's own noble efforts.

Here's an important tie-in to the comments of that talk-show host, who was willing to "stand by," which is an act of complicity. The host was an example of "passive" complicity, while Adam is an example of "active" complicity. Adam's sister did not want to be in passive complicity, and her actions caused her loss and pain.

Surely, her sacrifice was worthy, for Adam was moved enough to struggle with me over the issue. There would have been no struggle if she had been inappropriately "tolerant." Adam's sister did not do evil to him, she shunned him, which is a powerful tool in motivating others' behaviors.

However, some people don't act with such courage and conviction unless it comes back to bite them personally.

BUT . . . THE SERPENT HASN'T BITTEN ME

Michael, thirty-six, is the married, stay-at-home dad of a one-and-a-half-year-old daughter. "I'm married to a wonderful woman," he said with great pride. "This is about my sister. About a month ago I applied for a loan and discovered that my sister had used my Social Security number to get herself some money. Boy was I mad. I took care of it, but I'm so upset about it."

I asked him to get to the actual center of his upset: was it that she hadn't trusted him enough to ask for help up front? No. I asked him if her behavior were really a surprise? No.

"So, Michael, your sister has done these sorts of deeds to others in and out of the family?"

"Yes."

"You've known this?"

"Yes."

"Did you deal with her in any way about these ongoing bad behaviors?"

"No."

"Why?"

"Okay, okay, I knew she was a bad person. It just pisses me off that she was bad to me! I've always been the one to not give her grief about it. I guess I thought that would serve as my insulation, protection."

Oh, really? Tolerating wrong, bad, or evil gives you protection against it? Since when does a spaghetti strainer make good armor?

Kathlee had a different solution:

Dear Dr. Laura,

Tonight, thanks to you, I was able to make an intelligent decision re the character of a man I've dated twice. I'll call him "Dateman."

Dateman informed me he was giving up his six-year-old for adoption to the man (we'll call him "Affairman") with whom his wife had an affair some six months after the boy was born. Affairman and ex-wife have been living together since the affair and just recently married.

Dateman's reasons for giving up his son: "She's crazy. She makes my life miserable when I try to see him. I'm tired of fighting her. My son thinks of the other guy as his dad.

My response: "If she's crazy then rescue him! Go to court, you have the right to see him. Get custody if he's in psychological danger."

Dateman: "I don't have the money."

Me: "Get the money. Work two or three jobs if necessary."

He hung up on me saying "You don't understand" after I told him he was abandoning his son, that he was taking the easy way out and that his son would never forget his father gave him away.

My intelligent decision: He's weak, selfish, morally and spiritually lacking—so, I will not date him again.

P.S. He called me back later in the evening to thank me for speaking my mind. I asked him if he was going to do the right thing for his son. He said yes. Hmmm, we'll see.

P.P.S. I'm still not going to date him until I see how and if he's there for his son.

Letters like Kathlee's restore my faith. Here's a woman more passionate about the "right thing" than about romantic or sexual passion.

When you stand by and watch "wrong" and do nothing about it, when you get involved with "wrongdoing" or "wrongdoers," you are wronging yourself, family, community, and the moral values that have protected you in the past.

BUT . . . MY BED WOULD BE COLD

"I don't know whether or not to tell some friends that my fiancé stole from them," worried Judy, forty-six.

"Do you think you should protect those folks?"

"Yes."

"Do you think your fiancé should be punished?"

"Well, yes."

"Did you continue to have sex with him once you knew what he was doing?"

"Yes."

"Help me understand how you could be sexually turned on to someone you know is perpetrating felonies."

"I didn't really have a problem with that because I love him physically, even though I don't love some of what he does."

"You get off on his body, so you were willing to use it for pleasure and not really caring about what kind of person he was?"

"Yeah, that's right."

"Judy, who do you think is more despicable?"

"I think he is."

"Why?"

"Because I don't steal."

"You're willing to give comfort and aid."

(Long silence.) "Well, I suppose in some ways that's despicable."

"In what way is it not?"

"I can't think of any."

In computer-speak, this woman sounds like someone who never got initialized, that is, got booted up, with values.

BUT . . . IT'S JUST EASIER

Taking moral positions just isn't easy. That's what I hear a lot. You know, "People get mad at me" and such. I don't really understand it, though. It seems to me that not taking moral positions and knowingly protecting, supporting, or benefiting from wrong would be to the soul and psyche like flesh-eating bacteria are to the body. But, that's where excuses and rationalizations come in.

Greg, forty-eight, and Amy, forty-three, husband and wife, called in unison. Amy's best friend wants her own twenty-six-year-old son and his new live-in girlfriend with three kids to come stay with Amy and Greg because they don't have any money left and had to give up their apartment. Momma doesn't want to see her own son homeless.

"Young people in love against the world" is how Amy's friend describes the creep who skipped out on his wife and three kids under five to be with the new honey.

"What is the right thing to do here?" they asked. "We'd like to help, but we don't think it's the right thing to do. We really don't want to do this. It's hard having houseguests. If we allow them to stay, we will be helping them out."

"Greg, you seem to be very sympathetic, and I wonder why."

"We've been married twenty-seven years and have been through hard times ourselves."

"How can you compare your continuously committed marital relationship to his having hard times with a new live-in after dumping his family?"

"Well, he wasn't born with Dr. Laura wisdom. He's just a kid."

"Oh, Greg, you're excusing his actions? Well, if you really want to help out and be moral, take in his abandoned ex-wife and three kids and support them!"

They laughed. "We're not that moral."

"It seems to me that you are supportive of the wrong side here. Where is your support of the victim? I think that to you the real issue here is not moral action; it's that you've had this thrust at you by your friend and you want to look good, or at least avoid a confrontation with your friend about your unwillingness to help her son out—whether the reason is comfort or morality."

"Yeah, I guess that's a good part of it."

"I'd recommend they check into public assistance services or the resources of more immediate family. I think that it would be unconscionable to act in his behalf without first supporting his ex-family."

Let's not dismiss all the people who've been wronged and get all runny-eyed about the consequences of the perpetrator's actions causing themselves pain. There is such a thing as morally incorrect compassion; and dramatic concern for the well-being of these particular "young folk in love" would be a slap in the face to the abandoned wife and children. Since emotional and physical resources are limited, the morally correct position would be to aid the abandoned family first.

SLEIGHT OF HAND. . . . SLIGHT OF MIND

I feel sorry for anyone's pain and problems. But when they are the result of betrayals and abandonments coming back to haunt, and the primary issue is not remediation of those actions, I don't feel it to be an ethical obligation to get personally involved.

Trina, twenty-eight, has a sister, thirty-four, who split from her husband and has a new guy who dumped his wife. The sister kicked out her own seventeen-year-old daughter, who wasn't going along agreeably with all this and is now living with Grandma. Trina is now wondering about not inviting the live-in guy to a family event.

"Trina," I scolded, "you are displacing responsibility about this situation to him. You want to punish only him, but your sister is the one making the decisions; she chose him and she dumped her own daughter. Your sister's actions are being ignored so you can be appropriately, but safely, righteous? You don't want to upset the family applecart, right?"

"Right."

In discussing what her sister was actually doing wrong, Trina kept trying desperately to pardon her sister's:

- low self-esteem

- lonely

- beguiled

- not thinking straight

- confused

- lost

- etc.

Sure, Trina says the guy is a bum, but she's just as sure her sister is merely weak and confused, not really bad. How is that again?

In psychological terminology, Trina is "splitting," i.e., ascribing ever so neatly all the bad behavior to one person and all the good to another. This is a means of coping with the difficult ambivalence of having love and attachment you feel for someone and not wanting that to be marred by ugly realities.

Well, in real life, all good people do some wrong things and all bad people do some right things. I've heard many women defend abusing men by saying, "But, other than that he does good stuff!"

YOU ARE NOT WHAT YOU EAT . . . YOU ARE WHAT YOU DO

This brings us to the "bad person" *vs.* "bad deed" argument. When children are being taught morality, values, ethics, and character, they are often told, "You are a good boy/girl and I love you, but that action was wrong/bad." That is fair because the child is only now learning the notions of responsibility, selflessness, and goodness. Learning is trial and error until the good behaviors become habits and the concept of ethics is incorporated into the personality. Until then, good child–bad deed makes sense.

However, too many adult folks try to cop to that plea, implying they are somehow separate in identity or value from their acts and behaviors. I don't think so. I believe we are the sum total of all that we do, i.e., what we "do" is who we "are." This is true because as adults we make deliberate choices in our actions. Therefore, our actions describe our inner selves, what sacrifices we're willing to make, what evil we're willing to perpetrate. It is with awareness that we persist in negative, ugly, and destructive deeds in one or more areas. Our actions are the blueprint of our character.

Nonetheless, we sometimes try to avoid "naming" the good/bad by pleading ignorance, like the bill of goods Theresa, thirty-eight, tried to sell me.

BUT . . . GOSH . . . I JUST DON'T KNOW WHAT TO THINK . . .

"I have a situation that makes me feel real uncomfortable, I don't know what to think," Theresa complained.

"I can't let that go by. Not knowing what to think has never stopped a mind from thinking something. So, without your telling me the problem, I want to hear what you honestly think about it in one sentence, please. Start with, 'I think . . . '

(Theresa struggles, stutters for the longest while.) "I think . . . he's being dishonest."

"So in your heart of hearts and mind of minds you're sure that he's being dishonest. Do you know why the question was so tough to answer?"

"No."

"Well, for the sake of time I'll suggest why. You want to find out how to whitewash whatever it is he did so you don't have to lose him. If you have specific, firm, negative thoughts, it would be harder to stay, and you would rather try to make this okay than be alone."

"Yeah, but . . . "

"Theresa, just stay with this for a while. This one circumstance is not that important, but how you face these dilemmas in the future will define your life. Right now, your personal philosophy and manner of handling things is like warm Jell-O."

"I think I'm just indecisive."

"Nope. You know exactly what you think . . . but you won't act out on it because you want to keep him. Just because. So, instead of admitting what you know to be true, you go into, 'I'm confused.' You'd be better off functioning through what you know and believe to be true, pay the price of being alone, and consider it a reward and an opportunity to do better!"

Like so many folks, Theresa doesn't want to lose the imagined, minimal, or periodic comfort of the moment. This is the fundamental exchange: immediate comfort or gratification versus ideals that transcend comfort but build character.

I'LL SPELL TRADITION ANY WAY I WANT!

I remember one particular call from a woman who said she was an Orthodox Jew who was living with her fiancé. She was angry with his mother, who wanted them to move closer to her, which would mean that they'd have to drive to synagogue on the Sabbath, which is not permitted in the practice of Orthodox Judaism.

I couldn't stop laughing. I asked her how living together and having a sexual relationship outside marriage fit into her practice of Orthodoxy. Piqued, she insisted she had the right to decide how to practice her religion. I responded that she sure did, but whatever religion she was practicing couldn't be called Orthodox Judaism. I added she was being hypocritical by using that framework to condemn her mother-in-law-to-be, while she was not respecting its more intimate requirements. I suggested she was religious "for show" only.

An Orthodox rabbi wrote to thank me for my strong stand and to bemoan how many "religious leaders" were adapting the rules to fit what the populace was willing to do, instead of attempting to elevate the populace to the profoundly meaningful ideals of the religion.

BUT . . . I WANT IT BOTH WAYS!

Our country was built on protection of the individual. The individual's rights and freedoms form the conceptual foundation of the Constitution and the Bill of Rights. But when individuals value their (ever-changing) immediate desires and call them their "rights," they lose an important sense of "humanness" by putting aside notions of their responsibilities, thereby dropping into "animal" behavior.

A seventeen-year-old high school student in Southern California (*Los Angeles Daily News*, 1994), fought her expulsion from a Catholic high school after she was married in a civil ceremony to a twenty-four-year-old man.

The school officials told her she could finish out her

junior year but would not be allowed to spend her senior year at the school because she was married. She had wanted to be married in the church, but several priests declined to perform the service because she was under eighteen. The Rev. Gregory Coiro, a spokesman for the archdiocese said, "We don't perform marriage ceremonies for people that young. They don't last that long." Living in a marriage not recognized by the church "continually flaunts the moral teachings" of the Catholic Church.

As the archdiocese representative finally stated, "This is a matter of choices and consequences—a young woman who makes a decision that runs contrary to the policy of the school and now she doesn't want to accept the consequences of the decision she has made."

The girl's attorney was a well-known feminist lawyer who seemed more concerned with the gratification of her child-client's romantic desires than supporting the meaning behind the church's ruling, which is designed to help protect children from taking steps not in their best interests.

The attorney said, "Marriage is not a crime, nor is it a contagious disease. Why should she be treated as a pariah and an outcast and be denied an educational opportunity because of it?"

My answer is simple: this teenage girl understood the contract with the church and the church school before she made her choice. Even her attorney does not want to honor that choice by allowing her to nobly accept the consequences of that choice. I think her attorney shows her disrespect. I think her attorney is not helping her build her character.

There are millions of individual roads to immediate gratification, and they are mostly a "slide on ice" with slivers as the reward at the bottom. The roads to nobility of the human species are few and difficult, but true happiness and joy meet you at the top.

People report suffering a great loss when something of sentimental value is lost or stolen. That means possessions are not just defined by their purpose or price; objects become special because of the special meaning with which we arbitrarily imbue them.

Well, eating is just refueling bones, muscle, and organs, unless you surround it with ritual or prayer. Sex is just an acting out of a biological imperative, unless you reserve it for committed love and responsible reproduction. Life is just about personal survival until death, unless you act in ways which are altruistic, compassionate, and creative.

You see, values give meaning to life, and all its otherwise mundane aspects. When you behave in ways that give your life meaning, you are fully human. As you aspire to be more fully human, you deal with the facts of life with courage, you make choices with conscience, and by those acts you will be known as a person with character.

6

§

For Brutus Is an Honorable
Man . . . Yeah, Right
(Where's Your Integrity?)

Count it the greatest sin
to prefer life to honor,
and for the sake of living
lose what makes life worth living.

Decimus Juvenal

Is your word your bond? Do you meet your obligations? Do you stand true to your vows? Do you live by a code of ethics? Do you fulfill promises and pledges? Do you irrationally circumvent self-survival and self-aggrandizement to act with altruism and generosity? Do you struggle with issues of fairness? Do you mean what you say and say what you mean? Do you display loyalty and fidelity? If so, we can count on you—and that makes you joyously and predictably safe and lovable.

Brutus' pre- and postbetrayal suffering (having chosen Empire over the loyalty required of friendship) highlights the agony of divided or conflicting loyalties and the painful necessity of the ranking of values, which makes the burden of honor heavier, more difficult to reason and to bear. No matter the challenges to honorable behavior, it is a requirement of a meaningful life. As Cervantes wrote: "My honor is dearer to me than my life." Life without honor is subsistence.

Your commitment to honor is tested daily through temptations and seductive opportunities—mostly, no one knows or sees these micro-events of integrity. But what matter? You know. And therein lies the greatest pleasure of honor, your self-respect.

When I first began my radio/television career, every performance opportunity was a coveted possibility for fame and success. So when I evolved into being a regular, the only regular, on a local TV talk show, I was thrilled. One day the competing station's number one–rated TV morning show called to "steal" me away. Believe me, this would have been a big step up in terms of visibility.

I turned them down. I thanked that number one show for their interest and told them that I owed loyalty to the program I was on because they had given me such a wonderful opportunity. I never told the producers of the program I was on about the offer—although I possibly could have parlayed it into more frequent appearances, or even some special financial compensation.

Within the year, a third channel offered me the chance to do a pilot for my own show. Immediately upon hearing of this (when it was only in the "talking" stage), the program I had "honored" (unbeknownst to them) dumped me without ceremony.

It hurt.

It also hurt when, due to no fault of my own, the TV show was a no-go.

Second scenario: Three and a half years after my son was

born, I was aching to get back into radio, but it seemed impossible to get back on that track after the hiatus. Then, a very, very small radio station near my home offered me a midday program for very, very small wages. I was so grateful I could hardly spit. My son and I would be together all morning, we'd walk to the station, he'd stay at a play center while I was on the air, then we'd walk home and have the rest of the afternoon and evening together. It was a gift from the heavens.

The only request the station owner made is that I would not take time off his air to fill-in or audition on any other station. Wouldn't you know, the big talk station in town called for me to fill-in, midday for one week, as an audition for that fabulous time slot. This was the opportunity I had been waiting years for. But, I had promised.

Friends lectured me I couldn't let this opportunity go by; that I should play out my boss's bluff by just doing it—there was no way he would fire me. Or, better yet, they said, quit and take the chance of getting this incredible gig.

I lost sleep on this one.

Finally, I told the big station I couldn't come and audition because I had promised my boss I wouldn't. The executive with whom I was talking emphasized that this was an important opportunity. I assured him I knew it and was grateful, but that I couldn't go back on my word. I remember asking him if he'd feel comfortable with me in that job if he knew he couldn't count on my word. He skipped that, just pushed a little more, gave up, and we hung up.

Someone else got that job. I cried a lot and even had a few bouts of hating myself for what I cursed as my "stupid nature." I gave fleeting thought to just doing whatever it was to get ahead because my "style" wasn't getting me anywhere!

When I went into that state, my husband would ask me just one question: "Could you really do that?"

The answer, of course, was no.

Despite the anguish and frustration, I was left feeling rather proud of myself, and that pride is what I've held on to.

I'm very successful now, and I don't believe for a moment that my success is some kind of cosmic reward or payback for having been honorable (and goodness knows, I haven't been perfect). I cannot promise you that goodness will get you your dreams. But I can assure you that integrity is its own reward if what you're seeking is spiritual peace, a quality life, and quality relationships.

SO ARE THEY ALL HONORABLE MEN?

Honor, or integrity, is the personal moral code you impose on yourself as a means of becoming more fully human. It is more animal to compete to win with no regard for context. It is more animal to seek immediate gain or gratification with no regard for context. It is the conscious decision to question and consider context that connotes "human." It is the conscious choice of other over self that connotes "human." Ants who die building a bridge that allows other ants to safe passage over water do not choose this noble path; it is instinctive, therefore amoral. Morality requires making a choice. Where there is no choice, the issue of morality is moot.

It is imperative that you not relegate (and thereby segregate from your everyday life) issues of morality, ethics, fairness, and honor to the realm of the esoteric subjects for college philosophy classes or barely-payed-attention-to Sunday sermons. Attending to those issues on a daily basis will help you find your way when emotions threaten to become the one unbalanced force in guiding your behavior.

Here's an example: Janet, twenty-five, called just the other day, beside herself with frustration because of her relationship with a married man. Only thirty days after he and his wife separated (for reasons she's chosen to remain ignorant about) they met and have been passionate-ever-after. Except for the fact that five months have gone by and no divorce actions have yet been taken. And there are children involved.

Janet talked about her own short, sweet, childless, ever so amicable divorce, which became final at about the time she met her present honey.

"Janet," I suggested, "perhaps you're expecting his severence to be equally unprofound. Remember, you were 'only' married, he's a 'family.'"

"But, Dr. Laura, I've put so much time, effort, affection, and sexual intimacy into being with him and helping him extricate from his marriage. The waiting is driving me crazy!"

"You know what, Janet? He and his family need to work out their problems. The best conclusion would be for them to find a way to recover from this threat to their co-existence. The best conclusion is for these people to stay a family. Janet, I'm sorry to have to tell you this, but you're 'in the way' of this important process."

"But I . . . "

"Janet, you're doing something wrong."

(Silence. Long silence.)

Now, as a therapist I try to help people understand the complex motivations for their behaviors. In Janet's case they could range from Mommy or Daddy losses (for which she is trying to compensate by being the winner in this triangle) to relieving the guilt left over from her cavalier divorce by recruiting others to do the same. Yet, bottom line, it ought to be clear that it is wrong to be disruptive and destructive to another's marriage.

Janet's immediate dilemma wouldn't exist if she functioned

under the honorable rule: "Don't date married folks . . . it's wrong. Don't do things to hurt someone else's family . . . it's wrong." Her personal psychological concerns about bonding, intimacy, loneliness, guilt, etc., could then better be dealt with directly and constructively.

A healthier version of her call might have been: "I've got feelings of guilt about blithely bailing out of my marriage. And I feel motivated to get involved with this married guy to feel better. I don't quite understand all that's going on with me, but I know having this affair is wrong. What should I do instead?"

I'm convinced that with an intense emphasis on honor and integrity, many of people's painful "situations" or "problems" simply would not exist. I'm trying to help folks eliminate from their lives the pain over which they have control. And I'm trying to help folks see that the single-minded desire to be happy at honor's expense is a fast track to hurt.

REMEMBER, HAPPY IS ONE OF THE SEVEN DWARFS!

James Wilcox wrote in the *Los Angeles Times* (5/7/95): "The pursuit of happiness may be one of the inalienable rights guaranteed by our founding fathers, but it's not always a particularly noble nor a worthwhile pursuit."

The number one way we all try to be "happy" is to be "in love." Unfortunately, our typical expectation is that being in love will produce a perpetual euphoria, without ambivalence, without the need for any reinforcement, without any other input, without any efforts or sacrifice. Wrong. That's a mistake my caller Kathryn made.

Kathryn, twenty-one, was married two years and has a twenty-one-month-old son. "My husband was my first boyfriend, my first crush. We kissed in fourth grade. We met up again after I had broken up with a serious relationship. Within one month of that breakup we started to date, three weeks from that I was pregnant, got married three weeks after that in spring break from college. I was 'all in love with him,' you know, passion and all that kind of stuff in the beginning, and we didn't give ourselves time to get to know each other. I was so gaga over him I thought I knew him. I even fought with my mom. 'I know what I'm getting into,' I protested. But my parents told me I didn't have to get married just because I was pregnant.

"I love my husband a lot. I have lots of feelings for him, but there are many, many times I ask myself why I stay with him because I love him but I'm not *in* love with him. Also, my ex-boyfriend, Eric, is still in my dreams and thoughts. I want to know why."

"Why, Kathryn, you ask why? Because you are twenty-one, and married with a kid when you should be in school with none of the above. Real life is not always a blast, fun, passion-filled, etcetera. It is hard work, responsibilities, and familiar routines. If you'd done all this at thirty or thirty-five, you'd be more ready to face that truth and balance these realities from less of a gimme-gimme-happy-vibes point of view. Attitude, and perspective, make us 'happy' more than passion does. If you went off with the ex-boyfriend, in six months you'd be feeling about the same, wondering where the thrill went."

"I don't know why I think about him so much, though."

"Escape. With your ex you'd be a schoolgirl again, no responsibilities past your next term paper, no kids, no obligations, just dating and intense, dramatic emotions."

"I feel guilty for dreaming about him."

"I absolve you of your guilt about your dreams, you're not

responsible for them. You are responsible for calling or seeing him, though."

"I won't do that because I know I'm not supposed to."

"Right. This is where values and morals come in. You feel compelled, but you don't do it because you know it is wrong and destructive to what you have."

When I went on to tell her about making the "best of" the situation, this brought tears to Kathryn. Somehow, she took that to be a kind of death sentence, rather than a ripening to a sweeter state.

THE "BEST OF" ISN'T SO BAD!

A letter from Sue, who also married too young, clarifies the nobility implicit in making the best of things. Sue and her husband had experienced what seemed like all the pitfalls of making big adult commitments without the experience and maturity of yet being an adult. Sue described her talk with her husband:

> Later, we began to talk frankly about our feelings for the first time ever. Admitting we were both too young and immature to be married, and certainly too young to be making three babies in three years. We finally have grown up and we are so glad we "toughed it out." We were a match made in fantasy, but we fell in love somewhere along the way. There's nothing we can't and don't discuss these days.

A "disillusionment" phase with your partner and marriage, perhaps with life in general, is normal and even expected. This is precisely where commitment comes in, because for stability and perks to the individual and to society, marriage and family need to be for "better or worse"—not just for better or until a better offer comes along. Every great relationship is such because it suffered through the disillusionment phase, and other such "lows." In fact, it is the process of surviving the lows that bonds us closer together, and leavens what we call love.

> Dear Dr. Laura:
> I thought this quote sounded a lot like you . . .
> "Love does not consist in gazing at each other, but in looking outward together in the same direction." (Antoine)
> I can confirm that after spending the last six years of building my relationship with my husband of four years, that "gazing" is kind of fun, but it isn't truly meaningful until you've looked outward together though the . . . "stuff" that life throws your way!!
> *Love, Debbi*

The romantic gaze into each other's eyes is part of the very crucial infatuation phase of a potential long-term relationship; it keeps people connected long enough to develop a more meaningful, longer-term association, including respect, admiration, loyalty, and commitment. Maturity gives the individuals involved greater opportunity to recognize this truth. However, even mature types are challenged by the disappointment that comes with the waning of fantasy and the advent of reality.

It is not that romance, affection, and passion actually disappear. It is, rather, that they are now specific to real personalities and real situations and circumstances—and are no longer inspired simply by novelty, wishful interpretations, and blind sexual tension.

For example, when a woman first meets a man she checks out his shoulders, the laugh lines, the way he moves, his style of speech, the way he wears tight jeans, etc., and relates it to some ideal. That's the fantasy part. When she sees his underwear is faded or torn, the dream explodes.

If that same woman sees her man not replace torn underwear because he saved up to buy her a new watch, or that he canceled his business trip because their child has a karate tournament he refuses to miss, she is moved to a deeper passion of appreciation. This is the reality part.

It takes time to get from the fantasy to the reality, and honor and commitment are the forces that get you there.

The obvious immature alternative is to ditch your present reality and go for another, rationalizing that your partner must be doing or being something wrong or else you'd just be perpetually grinning. Oh, yeah?

Some people, the ultimately "lucky" ones (as Mae West so aptly put it: "Luck had nothing to do with it"), stick it out and end up with the satisfaction they were complaining about missing in the first place.

I'M OK, BUT YOUR WARRANTY HAS EXPIRED

David's letter affirms this reality:

> **Dear Dr. Laura:**
> I will sign myself, "A happily married, forty-year-old, Christian father of three daughters, ages six, eleven, and thirteen . . . and damn proud of it." However, while I am happily married now, that wasn't always the case. My wife and I will be married fifteen years in October. The marriage started off

good, but then things got steadily worse until it all came to a head about two and a half years ago. We had just gotten off a three-month grouch with one another when we had another big argument. This time I had had it. I knew that I couldn't go on in our relationship the way it was and began to seriously consider divorce.

There were all sorts of reasons to split up: our relationship was strained and distant, I knew our kids were suffering watching us fight, we couldn't talk anything out. Coupled with this was that a woman I knew casually made it very clear that she wanted to get to know me much better (she was in her mid-twenties, married, very cute and if she wanted me . . . well damn! I must be hot stuff!!!).

I knew I'd lose the house and most of my money to child support, but heck, it would be worth it!

Then I got selfish. I thought of what I'd really lose. Tucking my daughters into bed, reading to them, bathing them, wrestling or playing hide-and-seek with them. I thought of what playing the part of the Tooth Fairy and Santa Claus meant to me, of helping with homework and all the little things I'd miss if I wasn't there on a daily basis. Besides, if I was gone who would greet my daughters' first dates at the door with a hearty handshake, a smile on the lips, and a look in the eye that says "have her home by midnight or I'll hunt you down and beat the bejabbers out of you!"

In short, while I'd still be their father, I'd miss too much of what it was that made me their daddy.

So, I decided to stick it out and I got a new attitude.

I became more understanding of my wife's problems and more considerate of her. I tried to help more around the house and with the kids, not so much to impress her but to give her less to complain about. I didn't really expect much in return, but a funny thing happened. The more I did for her, the more concern she showed for me. And as our concern for each other grew, so did our respect. Just as our arguing had been escalating in the past, our love is growing now.

I am so grateful to have my wife and my daughters.

Sincerely, David

"AS IF" LEADS TO "WHAT IS"

David, moved by his commitment to be his kids' daddy, decided to behave, what I call "as if," which refers to choosing actions that create the positive result you have been wishing would materialize spontaneously. The important part here is acknowledging first that you really do expect the other person to create your perfect world, and second, how much you've done to make sure it can't happen. Of course, you won't admit to that. Instead you insist you would be behaving nicer, if only he/she . . . In other words, you interpret their bad behaviors as intentional and evil, and you interpret your bad behaviors as innocent, passive, defensive responses to them.

If that were always truly the case "as if" wouldn't work as often as it does. And it does work. Ask my caller Elizabeth, twenty-five, who wrote to me discussing her formerly bad relationship with her husband:

We argued most of the time. We never had sex, or any loving and touching, even hugs. My day was spent thinking of all that he should be doing or saying to get this marriage on the right track. Suddenly, I had a change of behavior, directly related to your teachings on the radio. I began behaving "as if." I spent my time being helpful to him rather than nagging him about being helpful to me. I told him any and every good thought of him, instead of shrieking how our marriage was rotten and a big mistake. I touched him every time I passed him, even a brush on the arm.

This is a brief description of my "as if" behavior. After one or two weeks, his behavior changed. He expressed love and appreciation for me. He became more helpful around the house. Low and behold, we are in love. We are happier than ever, even before we had a kid, a dog, a house, less money, etcetera. We laugh, we discuss, we hug, we have sex.

This is not to say we haven't had some lows, but instead of swimming in trouble, we both strive to get on top. We are committed to keeping things positive, helpful, kind, but most of all, we are acting in love. We will continue turning to you for ideas and guidance, and we are looking forward to many years, so don't go anywhere!

> *Thank you,*
> *Our grateful family*

Honoring commitments to family, children, spouse, and vows gives you the opportunity to build relationships of deep meaning. Relationships of deep meaning bring satisfaction and happiness. Honoring commitments brings satisfaction and happiness. That sounds like win-win to me!

It takes strength of character to accept real responsibility for your own perceptions, attitudes, and actions. It's a lot easier to affix external blame and/or give lip service to personal responsibility only to apparently clean the slate and leapfrog to the next fantasy.

"As if" behaviors force you to face how your own (in)actions contribute not only to your unhappiness, but to the unhappiness of others. Since no one really enjoys seeming like the "bad guy" for even a moment, many avoid this step to steer clear of fault or blame; in doing so, they miss the opportunity to create real magic.

ABRACADABRA . . . I'M HAPPY!

All magicians create illusions; the magic doesn't occur without their intervention, input, and creativity. You must be the magician in your life and relationships in order to have experiences that bring deep satisfaction. Sometimes your magic is definition and attitude—which the following letter conclusively proves.

> Dear Dr. Laura:
>
> I had to respond to a caller on your show yesterday. This man was complaining that after three years, he and his wife no longer had anything in common and that it was not "fun" anymore. This call really hit home.
>
> Over the past twenty years, I cannot tell you how many times it has not been "fun." This list of what we don't have in common is lengthy; for example, he would rather go camping, I would rather go to a five-star hotel. So, as you suggested to the caller,

I go camping with him and we also take wonderful trips together.

Now, when it isn't fun and I wonder what we have in common, I realize there is one thing: A life ... filled with three wonderful children, a long history, a deep commitment and endless devotion. As you perfectly advised your caller, if he doesn't hang in there when a relationship is no longer "fun" and interests drift apart, this is something he will never have.

A fan,
Diane

TEMPTATIONS ARE SUGGESTIONS, NOT COMMANDS

Sometimes people have to be urged into the "as if" mode. They know what they should do; sometimes they need to be nudged, nagged, shoved, or dragged kicking and screaming in the right direction because they're simply more motivated to find the "easier way."

I was frankly surprised when "Bill" (an alias) called to tell me he was revving up for an extramarital affair. Basically, he was giving me the power of first refusal over his actions.

"It just isn't sexy or exciting anymore at home with 'Peggy,' let's say. I'm entitled to some happiness, aren't I? And, who would know if I'm very discreet about it?"

I hit "Bill" with some pointed questions about his cooperation in the marital demise:

"So, Bill, do you sexy up to 'Peggy' like you think of doing to the new honey?"

"Well, no . . . "

"Do you court her with words of love and seduction and plan romantic or downright horny moments, events, experiences, opportunities . . . ?"

"Well, no . . . "

"Do you talk all warm and playful with her, like you would your new honey?"

"Well, no . . . "

"Maybe part of the boredom and letdown of your marriage is that you don't do what you used to, or what you'd do for a new honey."

"I didn't think of that."

"Here's something else. If you do something embarrassing in front of the new honey, is she likely to be as compassionate and accepting or helpful as Peggy?"

"Well, no . . . "

"With the new honey would you have movingly nostalgic conversations about life's special events? Or just where you 'made it' last time?"

"Well, no . . . "

"What do you think Peggy has done about the same feelings? Did she get herself a stud to make up for the boredom with you?"

"What?"

"Oh, you think you're the only one bored in this relationship?"

"I didn't think about that."

"Is it likely that in spite of the boredom of living with you not being romantic, seductive, playful, etcetera, that she's broken her vows and dishonored your trust?"

"No."

"Then, although she's stuck with you, she still has her honor?"

"Yes."

"And if you messed around on her would she still have her honor?"

"Yes."

"And what would you have?"

A while later I received a follow-up letter from Bill:

> I wanted to write to you and thank you for the help you gave me one day when I called your show.
>
> You may remember me, the name I used was "Bill" and my wife's name was "Peggy let's say."
>
> Without going through all the gory details, I was tempted to step outside of my marriage vows with another woman.
>
> Well, I am happy and proud to say the temptation has passed and I have you to thank for helping me through a tough spot. I have remained faithful to "Peggy" and because of this I think it has strengthened the bonds of our committment to each other (at least on my end; she still has no idea what has gone on and I am not about to tell her).
>
> I think that by going through one of these crises and remaining true gives one the perspective to avoid future situations like it.
>
> Again, thank you for your level-headed viewpoint about life.
>
> Warmly,
> "Bill"

How did Clint Eastwood put it? Oh yes, Bill "made my day!"

Tracey sent this poem; it gently gives closure to Bill's tussle with honorable actions:

I have to live with myself and so,
I want to be fit for myself to know.
I want to be able as the days go by,
Always to look myself straight in the eye.
I don't want to stand with the setting sun,
And hate myself for the things I've done.
I can never hide myself from me,
I see what others may never see.
I know what others may never know,
I can never fool myself and so . . .
Whatever happens I want to be,
Self-respecting & conscience free!

Author unknown

You see, character really is what you are when no one else is looking.

THE RIPPLE EFFECT

Donna, thirty-two, heard Bill's call, and it changed her marriage by changing her behaviors:

I was listening a couple of weeks ago when you told a man he should honor his wife because she remained faithful and honored their relationship. I have been in a marriage for seven years. My husband and I love each other dearly. I do have times when I will perceive him in a critical manner. I guess you could say that at those times he doesn't behave the way I think he should. When you made that comment to this man, tears came to my eyes, and I realized that I wasn't honoring this wonderful man in my life.

I have now found a way to curb my need to control him. Each time those feelings come up, I look at my husband, and I say to myself, "I honor you for being in this relationship with me. I honor you for being yourself in this relationship." That feeling of wanting to control disappears.

I make a point of honoring him at least once a day. I have become a more loving partner. I am constantly reminded of what attracted me to him when we first met. I admired him because he was always himself. Through the years, I began to look at him differently and tried to change him. Thank you for reminding me. You are truly an angel.

Love, Donna

So honoring a relationship has more than one profound meaning. For Bill, it was honoring the vows of fidelity. For Donna, it was honoring the integrity and the value of her husband, with whom she made vows. Actually, I think the two ideas must be inextricably intertwined.

The energies Bill was going to detour into an affair needed to go into his marriage. While his initial efforts may seem awkward and uncomfortable, the long-range impact would be subtly moving. Bill would not only have forged something deep and strong with his wife but also created more depth within himself. Character builds satisfaction in life in a curiously indelible way.

Donna's story brings up yet other familiar issues. She admits to being controlling; first she marries her man, then she tries to change him. Remember, control issues are about insecurity. Donna marries someone she recognizes (and envies?) for having the security to be himself. She then finds ways to demean and destroy that, in an attempt to not feel "less than," in an attempt to control outside of herself what she's scared to control and confront within?

From Bill's call, Donna followed the idea of honoring someone into its appropriate extension: respecting the integrity of his personhood. Recognizing this to be a necessity of intimacy, she came up with a behavioral modification technique to remind herself to respect him. In so doing, she gained the equivalent of years of therapeutic growth. Since her insecurity and her husband's security dovetailed anyway, she found a way to benefit from his security—by honoring it! It's amazing how unself-centered true personal growth really is.

The pop-psych notions of personal growth usually mean that others need to be brushed away like lint, as though others, more specifically our obligations to others, are like a straitjacket, constraining personal growth. Perhaps you might now begin to think of personal growth as a wine, sealed in a bottle, aging, and gaining value.

You see, the means do matter.

THE "MEANS" GIVE THE END ITS MEANING

How you get something ought to matter more to you than the fact of getting it. That's a lesson that needs to be taught from infancy. The letter you're about to read is from a dad who struggled with his own integrity and ended up teaching his boy about honor.

> Dear Dr. Laura:
> I really enjoy your show and feel I have gained from your example of dealing with people with a directness that cuts through the bull and all of the

"fuzzy" thinking, yet imparts an equal feeling of caring and compassion.

I am four years divorced and have worked very hard at developing the best possible relationship with my boys despite problems I have with their mother.

Your response to one of the callers this past week touched such a responsive chord with me that I got goose bumps—strange, huh? A married woman called in to ask how to handle a physical attraction to someone at work. Your response was that she had to do the "honorable" thing and not succumb to the temptation. When she said she agreed, but that it wasn't easy, you very eloquently pointed out that honor is not contingent upon ease or difficulty.

My oldest boy and I were having a discussion about the possibility of his coming to live with me, and this prompted a discussion about honor. I asked him if he knew what honor was. He said no so I told that it was doing the things that make you feel good inside and avoiding things that make you feel bad inside, without regard to how hard they were to do.

I asked him how he would feel inside if he didn't tell his mom and just didn't go back. He said he'd feel guilty and bad inside. I explained that that's because it wasn't the honorable thing to do. I also told him that my sense of honor would not let me be part of doing it that way, because it would make me feel bad inside to know that I contributed to hurting someone, even if I were angry with them to start with. I also gave him a couple of examples of times when I had acted with honor (and when I hadn't) and how it made me feel. The concrete examples seemed to help him.

I told my son that honor and responsibility were very important parts of growing up. We had a long discussion about how these character traits apply to one's life, from sex and girls to friends, to family, and to work. It felt so good to talk to him about these things because I got the sense for the first time that he really understood what we were talking about. Thank you for reading this.

From our words, but more deeply from our actions, our children learn what is expected of them, and that they owe people something—and that what actually "happens" in life is secondary to how you face up to those happenings.

HONOR MAKES YOU HEROICALLY HUMAN

If as a child you didn't learn about honor, there are still no end of serendipitous learning experiences to get you up to speed. One of mine was an unsuccessful attempt to have pet fish in an aquarium. One morning I noticed what I thought was mating behavior, one fish kept coming up under the other and lifting it up. Actually, the first fish was ill and the other fish was pushing it up to the surface. I began to cry, not only because one of the fish was suffering, but at the touching sight of apparent compassion.

The fish store owner told me something was wrong with one of the pumps in the tank, and that the fish wasn't really being compassionate because it was an instinctive behavior, not thought out. Well, the lower you go on the evolutionary scale, the less behavior is deliberate, therefore issues of morality are largely irrelevant; morality requires choice. Choice may embrace honor—*may*. It is in the quality of choices we make that we aspire to the title "human." In the following letter from Jane, we learn about one human being's struggle with a mate's illness balanced with her own desire for peace, quiet, and happiness.

Dear Dr. Laura:

I want to honor you for reintroducing the concept of honor to public discussion in your program.

My husband and I came to the brink of divorce three years ago, but stayed together. A year later he had a catastrophic brain hemorrhage, and although he survived, he's never been the same. The first six months were the worst, and I was surrounded by people telling me to leave him! I could never do such a thing, but didn't have an answer that didn't sound wimpy until I heard you talk about honoring one's commitments.

So "old-fashioned," so perfectly right. So now I have a way to voice my innate feeling that I could not cut loose a person in such a situation. What would I be teaching my children??? Run, when commitment gets tough? Heartless behavior is condoned if it gets you out of a difficulty?

Meanwhile, alas, my spouse now has cancer and life is still hairy to a high degree. Balancing the needs of a nine- and sixteen-year-old against those of a desperately ill man is tough. But I'm here for the duration, for all our sakes.

I hope my children will learn to make commitments cautiously (not impulsively) and then to honor them. Thanks for your help in spreading the word.

Warmly,
Jane

I think Jane is a true hero. She is basically sacrificing fun and apparent happiness. But she isn't whining or complaining because she sees her life as purposeful, measured by her honoring commitments *vs.* counting chuckles.

While Jane is sad for all the pain everyone is going through, including herself, and while she wishes things were easier and better, she cannot conceive of a bailout to greener terrain.

I THOUGHT HAPPINESS WAS THATAWAY

Some folks keep thinking happiness and inner peace is a place on the map instead of a state of being and behaving. Sometimes the lesson takes many years to learn.

Dear Dr. Laura:

Without going into too much detail, my situation is this: I am a thirty-one-year-old woman, and I have two children who don't live with me, my daughter, ten, and my son, seven. They have lived with their father ever since I left my marriage five years ago. My husband moved away and took the kids with him. I could have stopped him with a court injunction, but chose not to. At that point I wanted my freedom more than I wanted to be with my children.

Your emphasis on doing what is right and following the most ethical path even if it is the most difficult has forced me to see the strengths I didn't think I had, and also to acknowledge my past weaknesses. I have always loved my children, but let my own fears and immaturity keep me from fulfilling my role as their mother. And yet they still love me. The depth of that unconditional love just floors me, because I know I don't deserve it. I suppose my goal now is to behave in a way that is worthy of their love and respect. I have a lot of hard questions to answer when they're older, but at least I'll be there to provide those answers.

Thank you, Dr. Laura, for repeating the same messages over and over. And, finally, at least this one listener has heeded your words.

Gratefully, Sandy

I AM WHAT I CHOOSE TO DO

I'm remembering a 1995 syndicated comic strip, *Frank & Ernest*, where the two "bums" are sitting along a wall conversing. One says to the other, "Do you believe in fate?" The other replies, "Sure. I'd hate to think I turned out like this because of something I had control over!"

All sorts of political, psychological, social, and medical theories have been postulated to justify what people simply choose to do. The reasons for these classy cop-outs are many: political agendas (oppression as an excuse encourages shift in political power structures), good business (make something a disease and you can collect insurance for treating it or sell tapes and run workshops about how to recover from it), a need to disavow evil intent (we have no control over evil and thereby fear it out of helplessness), an inappropriate do-gooder mentality (not making anyone feel bad about "who they are" or "what they've done").

Nonsense! This is why discussions about honor and character must be brought back to the table. Essentially, people choose their actions and can alter them at will. The truth is as simple as that. Carrying out that truth tests our courage. It is easier to try to find a way to escape, to arbitrarily wipe some cosmic slate clean. I gave Kevin a going over for trying to do just that, when he told me:

"I'm thirty-nine. I'm living in with a thirty-eight-year-old woman for three and a half years. We met when I was divorced about a year."

"Kevin, why living-in instead of marriage?"

"We were building toward a marriage, but my last marriage of eight years split up because of a drug problem on my part. Once I straightened out my drug problem I had feelings about going back home because we have two children—two boys nine and eleven. I'm ambivalent right now. I don't know what to do, basically."

"Kevin, are you looking for the option that makes you feel better, the one that looks better, the one that has a guarantee of success? I need to know your criteria before I help you with this decision."

"I don't know, I love my children and my family life . . . "

"Do you hate your ex-wife, is she a bad person?"

"No, not at all. She is a nice person and she's willing to take me back."

"It's in your children's best interest for you to go back, stay and work through the discomfort and humiliation of facing up to having been a bum while you were married. A lot of people don't like to go backward and dig out from under the mess they've made; instead, a new person who sees them in a new light is a relief."

"Yes." (Kevin laughs, knowingly.)

"You have no prices to pay if you don't go back. If you do you have to make up for things, deal with some distrust and residual pain of your family members. It takes courage and honor to go back. Your kids will be better off if you go back and make the best life you can with them, even if your groin starts hungering for your live-in honey."

"You have such a way of putting things, Dr. Laura. But, okay."

"Kevin, some people define happiness by taking, others by giving, others by a balance of the two, others by simply having a good time, others by avoiding challenges, others by having challenges through which they stretch and rise to the occasion. Kevin, what kind of man are you?"

"I'm willing to rise to the occasion, but the question in my mind is that maybe you can't go back once it's done. Because people have told me that it never works when you go back."

"Depends why you go back. It's a question of guilt-only versus guilt-plus-commitment."

"Good point. Guilt . . . yeah . . . this has all been so hard on my kids."

"And what have they learned about being a man and a father from you? Drugs and a new live-in honey? What do you want to teach them now?"

"How to be a real man."

"Then, Kevin, role-model that for them."

When Kevin goes back to face responsibilities, his attitude will be everything. He has to go back knowing he's got a lot to make up for, and can't afford to get bent out of shape when everybody is just not the way he imagines they should be. He has to regain his kids' respect; he must regain his wife's respect, trust, and affection. It isn't going to be easy.

Actually, Kevin's decision to return to his family is the easiest part of his task. After the "honeymoon" period is over there will be challenges and expectations that seem upsetting and even unfair. He has to know that going in, and he has to be willing to weather them. Ultimately, all this can make him very happy, not just because he'll be reconstructing "the Waltons," but because he will come to admire himself much more through his own efforts than if some honey likes him in spite of what he's done.

STAND BY ANY MAN?

Kevin is willing to mend his ways, but some people never see the light, and some folks, like Joanna, will go ethically blind in order to stay with them.

Joanna, twenty-five, has been involved with a "I'll be divorced real soon" man for one year. They met in Texas, where his wife and child continue to live, but have recently moved to California. She complained about having given up home and school to follow him while it seems he really isn't pushing for the divorce. She wondered whether his guilt over having an eleven-year-old daughter might be the reason he's postponing the divorce.

I got on her case so bad!

"Joanna, explain to me why in your wildest dreams you would want to take into your life, home, and body a man who would physically and emotionally abandon his child? Why would any woman want such a man? Of what long-term use could he really be to you once you know that about his character? You are really calling me, all hot and worried, about actually getting the pink slip on this guy? This makes me ill."

Her response? "I guess I really never thought about it."

I'm frustrated with the kind of moral blindness that permits Joanna and so many others to give comfort and companionship to someone so dishonorable. I suppose that birds of a feather naturally flock together?

Supporting dishonorable behavior is not just a "girl thing," although I do think it is more typical for women to want to nest so bad that they don't really mind much what the boy bird has done to other nests. I guess they think that some miracle will protect them. Worse, though, they don't realize that what you "choose" defines what and who you are.

WHO WAS THAT MASKED MAN?

There are many men riding out of town with tearful little children asking, "Who was that masked man?"

Al, forty-two, has been divorced three and a half years and has three children eleven, fourteen, and sixteen. His wife divorced him because he was an absentee member of the family, choosing to travel a lot "for business." Of course, after the divorce, he stopped the traveling; that made his new live-in honey, twenty-eight, very happy.

"Al, why did you pick after the divorce to change your schedule?"

"Well, hindsight is 20/20. My girlfriend wants to leave town, and she wants me to go with her. I want to be real involved with my children. I even went to get physical custody of them."

"You were trying to take the kids away from their mom who was there day in and day out while you were on the road all the time? What nerve!"

"I was always there for them when I was in town."

"Oh, we're all happy for that, but she was the hands-on parent all the time. You've already lost points with me, let's see what we can salvage."

"I'm being honest."

"Just because you're honest doesn't mean that what you've done is right."

"I understand that. My girlfriend wants me to move with her to another state so that she can finish up her advanced degree."

"Isn't the answer no?"

"I would always be there for my kids, regardless."

"No, you can't be there for them when you aren't there physically on a consistent basis.

"Your first responsibility when you make kids is to parent them. That means everything else comes second. Why don't you tell your honey that she can have visitation with you every other weekend when she flies into town to see you. Give her some sense of what that's like. Do you think she'll think that you can "be there for her" when you're not physically there as well as when you are?"

"No, I guess not."

"It's easy to understand how the desires and affections of a young lady could pump up your ego, but if you get so carried away that you are blind to your responsibilities, you ultimately won't like yourself."

(Silence.) "I see . . . I guess it is clear-cut."

The right answers usually are. The difficult part is expediting them. That's where character and courage come in. True commitment is about behaving in the way you promised to behave, now that the mood in which you made the promise has changed. Motivation shifts from the external (immediate feedback and gratification) to the internal (conscience).

But what if the external motivation does continue, and quite negatively. Then what?

Steve, thirty-four, is having trouble dealing with a decision he made two months ago: he is giving up all visitation rights with his twelve-year-old son with whom he's been involved since birth. He wondered how to "deal" with the pain of that.

When I asked him to clarify whose pain, his or his newly abandoned son's, he said his. He came to this conclusion because, "It just got too difficult to deal with schedules and my ex-wife."

When I asked Steve if he and his son enjoyed their time together, he said it was wonderful and virtually problem-free. I then suggested that it was his duty as a parent to "suffer the difficulties" with his ex-wife for his son's benefit. Frankly, I believed that he's had legitimate complaints about dealing with the ex. It's just that he needs to continue doing what is difficult so that his son is not abandoned by his father.

"Continue to see him, Steve, and just continue to suffer what you have to put up with from his mother. Consult with some experts to find ways to deal with her more effectively."

"Ah, the problem is that I'm not the only one who is suffering. I've got a new wife and three other children. It puts a hardship on the rest of us. It has cost me too much money and emotion."

"It was a decision you two made to marry and make other children under these difficult conditions. Don't make your first child, your son, pay the price. You all have to make the best of a bad situation so that you don't abandon a child."

I am not insensitive or ignorant to the fact that there are "bad" people out there who callously and self-centeredly try to hurt the ex-spouse by playing the "child custody/visitation card." However, even where there is little post-divorce enmity, the reality of the emotional devastation to the children and the noncustodial parent is considerable. Ex-spouses often go on to new relationships and "family" situations. Nonetheless, you don't quit on kids. There must be no divorce between parent and child.

Committed marriages and responsible parenting need to

become the new norms; instead, we are beginning to tolerate what was once considered immoral or shameful as either an acceptable alternative or an unavoidable reality. That wouldn't be so if society reinforced the notion of obligations.

LET'S JUST CUT THE CHILD IN HALF!

Children in visitation situations, even ones whose parents "get along," are constantly subdivided in terms of attention, routine, expectations, locations, experiences, etc. Their stability is constantly threatened, despite the best parental intentions. It is a far, far better thing we do when we work to never put children in that position.

That brings up the question of "staying married for the children." The prevailing pop-psych attitude of the last several decades has focused on the adult's happiness and fulfillment of needs, mostly through sex, new partners, and start-overs. The rhetoric of political correctness, in support of self-centeredness, is "the children are better off with divorced parents than ones who were not happy."

Bull. First of all, the research doesn't support that position (I'm not, of course, talking about families with problems of violence and profound substance abuse). Secondly, a home with the tensions and problems of folks dealing with stages of life, challenges of life, realities of life is not a toxic environment for children. I'm somehow certain that in the midst of the Depression years, the average marriage was not continually romantic or passionate. If there were ever an era when the burdens of reality might stimulate notions of escape on a national scale, that would have been the time.

However, values prevailed. People somehow understood that life was tough but that physical and spiritual survival depended on attachments to family. Most people couldn't imagine not honoring their obligations, and believe it or not, the very act of honoring obligations was in itself considered pleasurable.

Staying in a marriage for the sake of the children ought to be a much more viable motivator than pop-psych types either admit or recommend. Most people benefit tremendously by sacrificing and caring for children—from the sheer enjoyment of "being there" at bedtime, school recitals, tearful schoolyard problems, and so on. And, as several letters in this chapter have clarified, "staying there" for these nobler motivations gives grown-ups the opportunity to live through and work through their own seemingly insurmountable differences.

Obviously, any contract is only as good as the "goodness" of the people who enter into it, be it marriage or issues of custody and visitation. Courts can dictate, mandate, and hold in contempt. But if the individuals in question have no integrity, and value licking wounds through revenge, they'll even find a way around a legal order to do what they want.

It is interesting to explore the breadth of what is a contract. So far I've discussed the obvious contracts made and then dissolved: marriage and parenting and custody/visitation. Let's now go to another, more contentious level: the moral contract. Too many in our society have attempted to eliminate any sense of moral contract taking place at "oopsie"—i.e., unintended—conceptions. Nonetheless, the moral contract often comes back to bite you in the rear.

READY OR NOT . . . HERE I AM

Randy just wasn't careful about where he put his sperm—so he had an oopsie. He's thirty-nine and is happily married with six daughters. When he was single, some sixteen and a half years ago, he had an oopsie baby with a young woman even though he had no interest in ever marrying her or in being a father.

Although Randy told his girlfriend to put the child up for adoption, she decided to have and keep the baby. Subsequently, they agreed in writing that she would move out of state and never bother him personally and financially as long as Randy never tried to be a part of the son's life. The problem is that all of a sudden she has now popped up demanding child support for the next one and a half years. Randy's at a loss about what to do.

Since Randy has never had contact with his son, he hasn't developed a relationship or a feeling of bonding to him. He feels as though he is only the sperm donor. And yet . . .

I pressed Randy for what his question to me was.

"Well," he replied, "part of me doesn't feel responsible or willing to pay anything, another part of me feels a moral obligation to pay."

I pointed out to Randy that when he and the boy's mother had sex, they were not taking responsibility for the potential contract (the child) they were making. And when they both decided some sixteen and a half years ago to part company, that was, to my mind, an immoral contract—completely ignoring the rights and needs of the child.

The moment that these two adults merged genitalia, in my opinion they entered into a "potential and imminent contract" that bound them together for life as potential parents. In their case the "potential" became "real." Whether or not Randy planned marriage or parenthood, he availed himself of the behaviors (sex) that get you attached. We have a society now that finds ways to ignore, deny, or retreat from that truth, predominantly through abortion and acceptance of single parenthood over adoption.

I pointed out to Randy that his son being an oopsie does not absolve Randy from moral responsibility. When I clarified that to him, he came back with, "But I paid a price by not being involved in the boy's life."

"Randy," I countered, "that was voluntary and very chicken of you. You didn't want the responsibility, you didn't want this to mess up your plans. You wanted it to go away."

"Yeah, Dr. Laura, that is right. My wife and I have discussed this situation and realize my decision was a moral issue more than a practical financial one. That's why we decided to talk to you."

"Randy, you have a son."

(Choked voice.) "Yes, that's right. Thank you."

LET THERE BE NONE BEFORE ME

Randy was fortunate in having a current spouse who considered the morality and responsibility issues without getting defensive, territorial, and selfish. Their family has just expanded and is in for interesting adjustments as the children find out they have half-siblings and deal with the circumstances that generated that reality.

Thirty-two-year-old Joe's situation is more devastating. Seven years ago he had an oopsie with a young woman and, like Randy, signed away his legal rights to the baby. The girlfriend got married, got divorced, and is now back asking him for help with support of the child. Joe is now married with one child and a pregnant wife. If he gives money to the oopsie, his present wife is threatening to leave him!

Risky though it is, I suggested to Joe that he call his wife's bluff; not too many pregnant women with a small child wish to be on their own . . . and I hoped she was one of them. I suggested that he tell his wife that he was irresponsible as a young man in producing this child and then dismissing it, and his responsibilities to it, from his life. Furthermore, he was to say that he is no longer the kind of man who would abandon a child, not his and not hers.

I hoped that she, feeling a sibling rivalry type threat from the "other woman with child," would come to understand that if she could trust her husband to honor his obligations to "his" child, then ultimately she would be more secure with him and his honoring his obligation to "her" child.

There is obvious irony here.

OHHHHH SEX

Instant sexual gratification, even more than politics, makes strange bedfellows—and even longer-lasting consequences. Sexual gratification, sexual attraction, sexual feelings are tremendously powerful inducements to behaviors that seem to propel us out of control of our good sense or values. This is especially true if you've already had great sex or unbelievably exciting ongoing seductive behaviors with someone. A kind of "obsession" sets in as your ongoing focus becomes the potential or actual gratification. That kind of excitement threatens to overwhelm one's willingness to make moral choices.

So-called old-fashioned behavioral ethics that dictated sex only within the context of marital vows, believe it or not, aimed at making an important compromise. If one has sex as an "introduction" to knowing, trusting, loving, and committing to another, the ongoing pleasure and comfort sex can bring is potentially undermined by the very insecure nature of such high-risk circumstances. Compare that to having sex as the culmination of knowing, trusting, loving, and committing to another. The chances for betrayal, boredom, disappointment, and estrangement are by definition greatly diminished.

THE CHAINS OF FLEETING FREEDOM

In addition to the threat of meaninglessness and loss inherent in casual or recreational sex, there comes the higher risk of sexually transmitted diseases (mix 'n' match partners) and oopsie pregnancies (most usually leading to abortion, single parenthood, or doomed shotgun weddings).

Let me get back to that term "meaninglessness." Of what importance to life is meaning really? Sex is sex, and if it feels good it's great . . . that's all that's really important . . . right?

Michael, twenty-three, feels bad. Last night he met a girl at a dance, they went to a motel, and they had sex. He claims the sex was pretty good, but would have been better if he'd known the woman and been comfortable with her. Now he's left feeling a strange combination of empty and ashamed.

Hal, twenty-one, admits that he told his teenage girlfriend that he loved her because "I knew that's what she wanted to hear. And if she was happy she'd have sex with me. One problem—she got pregnant and she insists on having the child. I'm suddenly smacked in the face with the awareness of how that moment of physical pleasure will now dictate the rest of my life."

For those moments of sexual freedom, a lifetime of freedom is compromised. When you become an accidental parent and therefore inexorably chained to someone you don't really have a profound attachment to, you're saddled with a lingering sense of guilt, shame.

SEE NO EVIL, HEAR NO EVIL . . . MEANS "NO EVIL"?

Hal, smacked in the face with the "bigger picture," acknowledged his responsibility for what was spawned.

Daniel, twenty-seven, isn't feeling shameful or trapped. He's feeling "hurt." He's known this girl for six years and they've been engaged for one. He cheated on her with other women—who knew he was engaged! He and his "fiancée" broke up for a brief time, during which she had a fling with a married man.

"I'm just so devastated and hurt that she could do such a thing to me."

I expressed my astonishment to Daniel that his call was only about his hurt that his "lady" had an affair when they were broken up, and not about any self-loathing that he had affairs while they were supposedly together. It seemed to me that the crux of his problem was that his territorial feelings were more important to him than his own character.

He struggled with that concept a bit, before retreating back into the pained victim mode. He did offer that he now understands firsthand the pain infidelity causes and that made him think about his own actions.

But here's the punch line: while Daniel has moaned to his whole family about his lady's "affair," he has not to this day let his family or his lady know about his philandering. Instead, he's keeping the power by being the pained victim.

Since he understood that our own pleasure-seeking can cause pain to others and sees that fact as a basis for judging the behavior wrong, I asked if it would still be wrong if the other person didn't know and wasn't hurt.

This must have been a good question, because he didn't seem to be able to respond.

The correct answer is it would still be wrong because honor and integrity are what you are when no one knows, no one sees, and no one hears.

BUT, THEN SOMEONE SPEAKS OUT

But when someone sees, and hears, ought they speak out? I am asked a lot about whether "snitching" is honorable. Here are some examples:

"My father, just out of a five-year term in prison for fraud, has forged papers and is, without education and certification, pretending to be a clinical psychologist in a clinic. If I turn him in, I'll be responsible for putting him back in jail. My family will be angry with me for that. Should I say something?"

I told this young woman that her father's felonious behaviors will put him in jail. Also, and she demurred, she was still hoping against reality that somehow she could talk him into being a Daddy Huxtable so she'd have the perfect family. I hope she's not holding her breath.

And another: "My wife's best friend is blatantly fooling around on her fiancé. I mean, she talks about it and everything. Am I supposed to behave 'normal' with her when we double-date or get together at someone's house? I feel like a co-conspirator if I do or say nothing. Yet, is it any of my business?"

The response: The choice others make in their behaviors is not within your control. However, the people you choose to befriend and the behaviors you choose to tolerate are a measure and reflection of you and of your character. Facing her off about her disgusting, humiliating betrayal of her fiancé (even if he knows about it and is perversely tolerating it) and letting her know that these are not the qualities you admire in a friend, therefore you do not choose to be social, is, in my opinion, the honorable way to act.

Yet another: "I have a friend who is married to a woman who is both an alcoholic and the driver of a school bus. I am uncomfortable with what she is doing, yet everyone will know it was me who turned her in. This job loss would hurt the finances of the family."

My reflection: Is it worth losing a friend to save a life? Is it worth challenging them to face the alcoholism directly in order to save a life? Is it worth their temporary financial discomfort in order to save a life?

HONOR CARRIES A BURDEN

The issue of loyalty to a friend over the greater good of other individuals, society, and morality is one people struggle with all the time. Mostly, I think, because no one wants to be labeled the "bad guy" for hurting anyone else's feelings, even a wrongdoer. And that is the card usually played by the bad guy— "How could you do this to me?"

Good guys have to realize that "bad guys" consciously make the choice to do "wrong," and that the only reason their feelings are hurt is that they get caught, not because of moral regret, not because they really "feel bad" about what they've done.

That said, doing the honorable thing is not clean, easy, or without price. One parent called me just yesterday with this worry. Past his backyard is a small park. He saw a group of adolescents doing graffiti. He called the police and they were arrested. A number of the teens played tennis or took dance class with his daughters. Several of their parents actually had the gall to call this man and complain about his "turning their children in," ignoring the reality that their children's behaviors were at issue. This parent was worried about the impact on his daughters if they lost some "friends"; he had second thoughts about his actions because of the social ramifications.

I told him to tell his daughters to anticipate some fallout and to help them learn that honor most often brings with it a burden and a price, to teach them that to shrink under that is cowardly and dishonorable.

But sometimes there isn't a bad guy . . . just people in trouble . . . and it is most honorable to be involved. One particular letter about this issue has moved me more than I can express.

YOU OWE EACH OTHER—AND I OWE YOU

Jim's dear friends, with two children, are getting divorced. Jim wrote to them:

> I'm sure you haven't reached this point without a lot of thought and feel there's enough pain and hopelessness that it's impossible to go any further together. I want to challenge this choice.
>
> I would first like to remind both of you of an obligation I have. Almost twenty years ago I had the honor of being in your wedding party. Of course we were all there to share in your happiness and be part of the celebration. The other function of the wedding party is to witness and hold accountable the two people making vows. I'm here now to hold you both accountable for the covenant you made to each other that day.
>
> I am personally familiar with some of the feel-

ings I think you're both having: "I really made a horrible mistake" and "I would really be able to make a much better choice now, given a second opportunity" and "I don't think I was ever in love . . . I just thought I was," etc.

There is absolutely no perfect marriage and the best of them require a ton of work and commitment. Yours is no exception. Mine is no exception. All those expectations of marriage and romance can go very differently than you dreamed, and when they do, you are left standing at the crossroad where you are now . . . with the conscious choice to either cut and run, or do what it takes to stay the course.

The letter went on to create the real and painful picture of the divorced, single life, with the complexities and complications of family and child visitation and finances and more.

I was deeply touched by the character of this man, honoring his responsibility to his friends' vows, and charging (as well as offering support) his friends with that same duty. There should be more such "pressure" to support people's efforts and will to work through the bad times.

When individuals give themselves the permission to do anything they want any time they want, they will ultimately be alone. For it is in the obligations to others; the integrity of our beliefs and actions; our regard for agreements and pledges; our sincerity; the bond of our word; our honesty; our conformity to right and good; our fairness; and our inability to be readily influenced away from these character traits by the seduction of exciting momentary gain that others come to be comfortable and secure with us, and therefore love us. Then we are never alone.

7

❧

Eenie, Meenie . . . Ohhh, I Hate Decisions

(Where Are Your Principles?)

Guess if you can, choose if you dare.
          Pierre Corneille, 1646

Perhaps, in a curious way, the prior chapters are but a prologue to this chapter, for ultimately all the highfalutin talk about philosophy, values, morals, and conscience is reduced to that moment of truth when you choose an action, or inaction.

In the early summer of 1994, Connie Chung was relieved of her duties as co-anchor of the *CBS Nightly News* with Dan Rather. For at least a year media assessments had been made that Ms. Chung was going more and more "tabloid" on her magazine programs. Only after her termination did we read of the terrible pressures that had been put upon her to do less hard news and more popular and exploitive stories in an attempt to jump-start ratings on her failing *Eye to Eye* program.

Having experienced various aspects of the television

industry for some twenty years, I thoroughly believe she was pressured. But so what? I think of "being pressured" as an issue of a strongly given, maybe even threateningly delivered invitation, but certainly not a command with no options. Connie Chung, and everyone else in her position, always has a choice between personal and professional integrity and selling it out.

I'm here to tell you that choosing personal and professional integrity often brings with it a great external price: demotion, firing, even harassment. But choosing personal and professional integrity never brings with it a great internal price: shame, guilt, regret, and self-loathing. The external price can be responded to legally or with a change in venue. The internal price is indelibly etched into your soul and character.

In John Grisham's novel *The Rainmaker*, an important female defense witness uses the opportunity to testify against her former employers as revenge for her own choice in making an inappropriate, and perhaps illegal, invitation seem like a command. She had worked for a law firm where she was propositioned first by one boss, and later by another. Promises (not threats) of promotions and salaries went along with the exchange of sexual favors. In each case she agreed to use sex to her advantage, yet on the witness stand she whimpers and cries about having been a victim; after all, she is a single mother and needed a job.

Oh really? Since when did marital status and the universal need for food and shelter negate one's requirement to act with integrity? This character had the power of choice, made her choice, and now is trying to make someone else responsible for that choice. The bosses were wrong for offering, and she was wrong for accepting.

While the objective choices (loss of job *vs.* loss of personal integrity *vs.* lawsuit for harassment if loss of job happens) aren't desirable, we are all still charged with the freedom and responsibility to choose. Once that choice is made we cannot, by definition, call ourselves "victims"; the act of making a choice defines our freedom.

Granted, the support and sympathy you get from calling yourself a victim temporarily distract you from the inevitable pain of acknowledging your own weaknesses and inappropriate choice—all of which consitutute personal responsibility. But, my friends, you still must face the fact that something more than circumstance determined your predicament; you know you made a choice. It is only in humbling yourself to that truth that you become free from the internal hell of guilt and regret and become empowered to be and do better.

BUT . . . I WANT TO BELONG

This is all so blatantly right and seemingly simple. Why is it such a challenge? Why do so many people agonize over these decisions? One reason is the innate need of people to belong, to be attached to family, friends, groups. There is comfort, safety, security, and identity in belonging. That can be a good thing if it means belonging to the Red Cross, for example. That can be a bad thing if it means belonging to the purported Japanese terrorists, Aum Supreme Truth, for example.

Earlier in this book I wrote about how behaviors are selected for or against by the pressure of the group (family, community, etc.) in terms of group acceptance. These group pressures help direct us away from the self-centered into the other-oriented, thereby earning us approval and admiration. But we must always factor the concept of "balance" into the equation.

History shows us that group passion, unchecked by rational discourse and individual conscience, can easily lead to the lowest common denominator of human behavior: check out mobs, gangs, cults, ideologically adamant advocate groups, and the like.

People often permit themselves to be overwhelmed by their cowardice; their need to fit in somewhere; opportunities to inappropriately vent rage; displacement of responsibility; and their desperate desire to seem important if only by the exercise of raw power—sometimes malevolently rationalized through a distortion of religious values and obsession over survival.

According to the *Los Angeles Times* (5/21/95), "Several members of the doomsday cult Aum Supreme Truth have reportedly admitted to participating in the attack that killed 12 people and sickened more than 5,500. Some are said to have described how they made sarin nerve gas, and others to have admitted they carried out the attack."

Of profound horror is the more personal account of a physician, Ikuo Hayashi, who actually released the deadly gas in the Tokyo train. "When I looked around, the sight of many commuters leaped to my eyes. I am a doctor. In theory, I've been working to save people's lives. I thought, 'In spite of that, if I release this sarin fluid now by puncturing the bag with the tip of my umbrella, many people could die at once.' Tormented by pangs of conscience, I hesitated and thought a number of times that I should stop. But I couldn't go against the [cult's] orders."

This doctor knew he was doing "wrong," but that became secondary to his being part of a group. He sacrificed conscience for companionship.

Lest you sink into total despair, there are many glorious stories of character, courage, and conscience ultimately prevailing; where "belonging" is an attachment to an ideal, not protecting the evil in power. Many such stories are immortalized in the 160-minute Holocaust documentary called *Tzedek: The Righteous* by the French writer Marek Halter.

Through the simple and often emotional testimonies of thirty-six men and women in fourteen countries, Mr. Halter slowly builds his case: good can survive even in the most evil of circumstances.

"I could never accept the notion that the whole world was against the Jews," Mr. Halter was quoted in the *New York Times*. "I could not accept philosophically that there was no good, no generosity, left in the world."

"His evidence," the *Times* continues, "is the reason these 'righteous' [gentiles who risked their lives to protect Jews from arrest, deportation, or death during WW II] gave for saving Jews: 'because it was the right thing to do'; 'because I would have been ashamed if I had not done so'; 'because I am Christian'; or, 'what would I have told my children?'"

It is not a lack of fear that motivates this honorable behavior; it is a determination to be human. I don't mean human in the strict evolutionary sense of Homo sapiens. I mean human in the spiritual sense that elevates us to a plane higher than the tangibles of reward or loss—that of character.

BUT GOODIES I CAN TOUCH . . .

I'll admit it's a tough go to try to sell someone on what they can't feel, like values and character. It's easier to get someone's attention with the concrete, like immediate fun and avoidance of rejection. Let's be honest, a real experiential thrill is a high you can describe in mouthwatering detail; a moment where values are honored instead brings on a dead, stone-cold silence.

What then could we possibly use as incentive to choose,

eenie-meenie, and end up with values? Mike, twenty-seven, called with this dilemma.

Mike and I began our conversation with his denial that this issue tweaked any feelings in him at all; he said he'd been brought up not to express feelings. I worried aloud about the danger of not internally acknowledging feelings such as guilt, shame, regret, and pride, without which our decisions are made more from expediency than honor. It was then that he cautiously acknowledged that a coming decision might, just might, end up hurting his feelings.

To avoid getting mucked up in "details" I suggested we talk about Mike's dilemma without ever revealing the specifics.

"This is something I would kinda want to do, but . . . "

"Mike, do you think this is the right thing to do?"

"Yes."

"Then, when you have kids you are going to recommend this for them to do?"

"No."

"Then how can it be the right thing to do if you wouldn't tell your kids to do it?"

"Hmm."

"So, you know it's not the right thing to do, but it's adventurous or something like that and you'd like the experience?"

"Exactly."

"Mike, do you believe that after you do this thing you would admire yourself?"

"No, I don't think I'll admire myself."

"Then, why would you choose to do something you wouldn't admire yourself for? What would be the point? What could be so good that it would be worth that price?"

"Yeah. And I do stand to lose some things, too."

"So, it might be fun and adventurous, but there is some

potential loss attached to it. You could be hurt, you'd be ashamed to tell your children, and it would diminish you in your own eyes . . . "

"Correct."

"So, what's your decision . . . are you going to do it or not?"

"I'm not going to do it."

"Thank you for your call."

"Thank you."

Does it matter what the specific dilemma was? I don't think so. And not using the details as mitigations and rationalizations helps keep you focused on what you'll have to live with over the long haul: the long-range consequences and the state of your conscience. That is the primary tug-of-war: the immediate desired gains or avoidance of undesired losses *vs.* the longer-term, sometimes barely foreseeable issues of responsibility and honor. That's precisely why character requires so much courage.

I work to focus my on-air dialogues on the essentials of right and wrong and pride and guilt and shame, because it brings the future to the now—where it can more adequately compete with the expediency and excitement of temptations. In this way conscience is now introduced into the decision-making process.

OHHH, IT WAS CLOSE!

Remember when you were a hungry, growing kid and you wanted to eat something *right now!*? Your mother would probably tell you to wait until dinner and not spoil your appetite for good nutritious food with that revered "junk food snack." Nonetheless, which seemed more interesting to you at that very moment: the vegetable-laden beef stew later (Well, it will build bone, muscle, and good health), or that candy bar right now (Yeah, it melts in my hands, on my shirt, in my mouth . . .).You don't even have to answer me. But the stakes weren't that great then as they are now. Ask Darrin, thirty-six. He knows a lot about the price of giving into the "now."

Darrin works in a large hospital. Recently, a woman whom he's known very casually in the past was assigned to share an office with him. He writes that she is thirty-one, attractive, and married with a thirteen-year-old child. To make a long story short, Darrin and his officemate became mutually attracted. One behavior led to another, and soon they were doing the kissy-touch-feely at work.

"That's where you, Dr. Laura, come in," goes his letter:

> During my fantasizing about this woman I started thinking about some of the advice you give to people that are in the same situation. Well, I would like you to know that my testosterone is no match for your wisdom and advice. My woman friend and I had a nice talk about our own situations, and needless to say, common sense, respect, and cooler heads prevailed, all without the benefit of a cold shower.
>
> I was worried about becoming a caller to your program . . . "Hi, Dr. Laura, I am having an affair . . ." and the tongue-lashing I'd get because I didn't follow your advice, and it made me think about my actions before I did something I would regret.
>
> I still care very much for this woman, and I know she feels the same way about me. But even more important is the fact that I have a good friend, a good relationship with her, and a good healthy fear

**of a radio personality that helped me from becoming
the "One Stupid Thing That A Woman Did To Mess
Up Her Life."**

What actually kept Darrin from following through on his
temptation? It certainly wasn't that the opportunity lost its
appeal, or that the other person withdrew from the scene. It
was that he measured his potential and current actions against
a framework of values he respected, namely me, and his side
came up short. I had temporarily become his Jiminy Cricket,
his conscience.

All cultures introduce concepts of the "ideal" against
which to measure and choose your actions. "In the image of
God" does not refer to eye color. It refers to qualities to emu-
late. Many cultures encourage behaviors that do honor to
ancestors. Religions have commandments. Families have rules
and expectations.

Ultimately, individuals internalize these edicts of right and
good and perhaps holy. That is their conscience. It is there to
be used for guidance. When one's conscience is ignored or
bypassed with details purported to make their circumstance
different, there is hell to pay both internally (guilt) and exter-
nally (shame and/or the law). When an individual doesn't feel
guilt, our society has a sociopath on its hands; only good people feel guilt, only good people learn from guilt.

It is also amazing how far people will go to squash their
guilt, using terms like "happiness" as justification.

BUT . . . BEING GOOD DOESN'T MAKE ME HAPPY

Carey, thirty-five, married thirteen years to her high school
sweetheart, with three children, eight, eleven, thirteen, met a

guy. She's been having an affair with him, and she's over-whelmed with guilt, but she's thinking she deserves happiness. Her husband isn't bad, it's just that the lover is so good.

"I'm torn between my happiness and doing what I'm sup-posed to do," she cried.

"Do you truly see yourself happier after tearing your fam-ily apart; not just your immediate family, but all the aunts, uncles, cousins, and grandparents?"

"No."

"Do you truly see yourself happier after taking the kids away from their daddy?"

"No."

"Do you truly see yourself happier when the excitement of the affair mellows into the mundane of everyday life?"

"No."

I left her at this point in the conversation, asking her to rethink what she was sacrificing for a shallow definition of happiness.

In 1995 the PBS program *Frontline* chronicled the damage done to children by divorce. Among those interviewed was researcher Sarah McLanahan, a sociologist who had set out to prove that children raised by single parents were just as well off as those raised by two parents.

The results of her studies shocked her, because she found she was wrong. Children raised by single parents were twice as likely to be high school dropouts, give birth to out-of-wed-lock children while still children themselves, develop drinking problems, and have a higher rate of divorce when they marry.

In one segment of the program, Dr. McLanahan (a single mom) faced a group of women's studies teachers and researchers—which to my mind means a group dedicated to ignoring realities simply to justify their own actions and obfuscate their inadequacies and fears as women. Naturally, McLanahan was met with hostility: "If what you say is translated into policy, couldn't it lead to the loss of freedoms that were very hard won?"

McLanahan's reply (Mona Charen, *Orange County Register*, May 22, 1995) was "simple and elegant. She said yes. Freedom and family commitment are mutually exclusive. You do surrender some of your freedom when you undertake the care of children and promise fidelity to a spouse."

Not everyone, however, sees this choice as a loss.

> Dear Dr. Laura:
>
> I really admire your using your position to help parents see how important it is for "them" to be the ones raising the children they created.
>
> I am a twenty-four-year-old mother of two boys, three years old and five months. I have been married for five years. When we decided to have a baby I got pregnant immediately. I thought I could and would want to go back to work. Ha-Ha! I tried for six months too long. I was tortured, my son was tortured.
>
> I brought him into this world. I wanted him, he didn't ask to be born to be sent to a baby-sitter, a nanny, or a day-care center. I quit work, "gave up my career" and went through a lot of crap to do so. But I have the treasure of being with my boys as they grow up.
>
> IT WAS THE BEST DECISION OF MY LIFE!! I love being their mama.

BUT . . . I WANNNNT IT, PART II

Where the radical feminist types got off track was in their determination to make life "unisex" (that required denial of biological and psychological differences between men and women), and in believing that since money was power, nothing should stand in the way of a woman's attainment of it—not children, not family. The worst part of their agenda-maintenance behavior is an absolute refusal to acknowledge, much less challenge, any all-too-typical stupid behaviors of women; it is as though all the good in the many decades of the movement will be lost if anyone points out negative female traits.

I think the unwillingness to confront many women's inherent lack of character, courage, and conscience diminishes respect for the women's movement and ultimately diminishes women's possibilities.

An example of that is how women's groups defend repetitive out-of-wedlock births in single mothers, even those on continuous welfare, as their "reproductive rights." Rights? Yikes! Demanding rights without the assumption of balanced responsibilities is for toddlers, not grown-up women.

The following letter really got me going on-air. It is from a clearly good person with, to my mind, a clearly bad idea.

Dear Dr. Laura:
I have listened to you for years. Through your views of child-rearing I have gotten over my own childhood problems and more importantly my fears of having my own children.

However, today on your program you took that away from me. Because I am a lesbian and have been in a relationship for five years now and am preparing to buy a house this year and have a child the next year. This is the first time in all the years of listening to you in which I disagree with you. You said that "Lesbians should not make babies, but could adopt older children who are homeless; that in the adoption they get a home and love, even if it is not the ideal of a two-parent heterosexual home, it is elevated in position from where they were, without any home at all."

The father of my child, which has already been selected, is my brother. He said it was the greatest honor I could bestow on him. He is a pilot who could come and see his child anytime he wishes.

Sure there are lots of things we would have to be extra sensitive to . . . I could go on and on and on but we would do whatever would be best to help the child to grow up in the proper environment. I don't understand how you could ask me to give up such an important part of life and love (having a child) in the best family unit I could provide.

> *Sincerely,*
> *Donna*

When I get letters like this, from obviously decent people, who mean to be and do their best, it hurts me to realize how much the issues of decision-making and the role of values in prioritizing options can be hurtful. Nonetheless, I have a simple guideline: what is in the best interest of the child? And, while unavoidable losses like the death of a parent do happen, do we go out of our way to build in loss?

In this case it is the uncle who would be the father, peeking in now and then out of curiosity. Why is it that so many people see fathers and men as dispensable to a child's welfare? This child is condemned in the planning to not having a hands-on daddy. This is a good thing?

Also, since the child is likely to be heterosexual, how does this household arrangement of two lesbian women help with that socialization, much less present the masculine and feminine models, with which and against which children develop their full sense of gender identity?

This is not an anti-women or anti-lesbian statement; this is a pro-child statement. The most responsible and ultimately loving act you can make is considering the consequences to the child first—before the fulfillment of what you wannna have or think you have a right to have.

Since women are responsible for their own bodies in which the miracle of new life takes place, I hold women accountable for making the decisions to have children with men they barely know; are only shacking up with; not married to; have a lousy relationship with; guys with serious substance abuse and character problems, you name it. Then these women call all upset that sex didn't turn fairy tales into reality, that they have to share custody time with someone they now hate, or, worst of all, that the guy is totally uninvolved and their child is in pain.

These calls leave me in pain.

TO BE OR NOT TO BE . . . A DADDY

Becoming a parent is probably the most important choice we make in life. However, it is not the rule that people actively choose that option. From the calls I get, parenthood seems too frequently to be determined by . . . oopsie. However, when an "accident" happens in the context of a healthy marital situation, it is an honorably met challenge that ultimately brings a deeper joy to existence.

Of course, it's the responsible folks who agonize most over the magnitude of the parenthood commitment. A very worried Mark, thirty, began the call by assuring me he was happpily married but deeply conflicted about the decision to parent. Mark's fears of becoming a daddy included:

- fear of the unknown (what it would be like, how would things change, etc.)

- fear of being an inadequate father (doing it "right")
- fear of not much looking forward to the work involved

I was rather pleased with Mark's call. It brought out the agony of responsible decision-making. His concerns were realistic—and universal! He recognized the sacrifices required, and the challenges to be met and was willing to acknowledge the ultimate limitations of us all in attaining perfection in parenting.

We didn't end the conversation with Mark making his choice on the air. I validated his concerns but explained that the way each of us gives life meaning, and gives our own existence meaning, is to extend ourselves past our fears, challenge our limitations, and take on difficult tasks that touch our humanity—the willingness to sacrifice and demonstrate compassion.

There is no real, cognitive way to allay all fears and be totally prepared in advance for each detail of a commitment. If you wait for that in order to make a decision and act on it, you are lost. It is your philosophical view of the life in general and of this particular part of it (parenting) that opens the door. We then walk through that door and learn how to be more than we were. It is in such endeavors that we enhance our humanity.

WHY ASK WHY?

It is amazing how when we see the "bigger picture," we are less flummoxed by detail. I also believe that there is a limit to the value of investigation of details and all "why" questions— you can virtually drive yourself into an ethical paralysis by worrying through every real and potential detail of a situation. This letter from Barbara, twenty-eight, makes that very point:

> Dear Dr. Laura:
>
> Yesterday, you spoke to a girl who was overweight and trying to figure out why she couldn't keep the weight off. You said she should stop trying to figure out why and just take the action needed to lose the weight.
>
> It reminds me of a relationship I was in for almost a year. It was a horrible experience I allowed myself to be a part of. This guy had a girlfriend, yet he called me every day, we slept together regularly, and he took me out every week on a date. I thought I was in love with him. Yet, when I'd ask him where I stood, he'd always tell me we weren't boyfriend and girlfriend; we weren't "seeing each other," and we weren't lovers. He said we were just "friends," plain and simple.
>
> I never felt good enough and spent many hours crying and miserable when he wasn't there. I ended up in therapy trying to figure out why I was hooked on this person and couldn't stop the sex. I knew he was untrustworthy and noncommittal. I knew in my heart he'd make a terrible husband. Yet I hung on thinking somehow he'd pick me. Fact is, I really didn't want him.
>
> I spent so much time trying to figure out WHY I was allowing this to happen—nothing changed! Change only occurred when I decided to take ACTION.
>
> I took a beautiful vacation in my car ALONE. I

signed up for classes that were of interest to me. I made plans with forgotten friends. I basically tried to become the kind of person who I'd like to spend time with (not some unhealthy, needy kind of person with no hobbies or interests and nothing to talk about except a man who used me for sex).

Well, it worked. I broke away from the person whom I LET make me crazy. It wasn't easy, but I just stayed focused on the person I wanted to become. I met other nice healthy people. I ended up three years ago meeting someone to whom I am now married in a happy, fulfilling interdependent relationship.

It made my therapist angry. My therapist had suggested my going to co-dependent meetings but I refused because I didn't want to become the thing I was trying not to be and didn't want to wallow in what I had been. I could have analyzed to death why I let myself stay with that man for a year. Fact is, I don't care. I just stopped doing it and worked hard on becoming the person I wanted to be. It wasn't easy, but staying focused gave me the ultimate reward—real happiness. I'm so much more at peace now because I changed myself.

Thanks for being there.

What impressed me about Barbara's letter is that she was willing to forsake the sometimes interminable psychotherapeutic ruminating about the past and reach out with courage to build a stronger character. What so many people mistake for psychological "problems" may really be a reluctance to do the work it takes to become a special person who would enjoy and attract the special people.

There is no doubt in my mind that the combination of innate personality traits and the challenge of early family history can make this expedition more or less difficult. Nonetheless, it is the expedition each individual must make to have a quality life.

As Christina wrote: "The more time we spend blaming the past, the more time we waste. 'Cause while we were blaming, we could've been doing!"

HISTORY IS NOT DESTINY

So much of pop-psych literature gives the impression that people with difficult or ugly histories are somehow indelibly etched; hence the perpetual identification with survivor, victim, adult child of something or other, and lifelong membership in a never-to-be-recovered group. I worry about how the misuse and overuse of the above is actually helping people fixate in the negative and in yesterday, and in the "understanding" of why they aren't being and doing more.

Call me a heretic, but I believe that even with bad stuff in your past . . . you have choices! You need to activate your courage and move on. Of course, the typical argument to that is, "How dare you blame the victim for their unhappiness?" I think there is a big difference between blaming the victim for the actions of others and trying to get across the fact that perception, adaption, and action are in their power now.

> Dearest Laura:
> You are my role model, my surrogate mom. I am thirty-one and finally a light bulb went off in my head that yes, even though I had an unhappy childhood, and even though my parents could have used a

class in Parenting 101, and even though they'll never change, you put a thought in my head: "I CAN CHANGE."

Sure, I still sometimes wallow in self-pity, but I've made some life changes under your guidance:

1. I enrolled and completed a parenting class. I have no children yet, but my wonderful husband and I, after four and a half years of marriage, are finally trying to conceive.
2. I am taking guitar lessons, something I've always wanted to do but never put in the discipline to practice.
3. I am now an active member of the League of Women Voters, because I love politics.
4. I am a volunteer for MADD, so I can start thinking about others instead of only my own woes, and make a difference in someone else's life the way you have made in mine.
5. I have learned to be okay about being alone when needs be; this way I'm not a drag on others. I keep myself busy reading, playing guitar, keeping in touch with friends, baby-sitting, exercising, etc.

I worked hard for me but want to say thank you for your words of wisdom, which pointed the way.

Beth, thirty, wrote to me about her repeated molestations by both a stranger and a family friend, her parents' divorce when she was six, her virtual abandonment by her father, and the poverty that kept her from college. She wrote that "under these conditions, I could have become a 'victim,' but I chose to change my circumstances through hard work and perseverance. While some of my decisions were indirectly related to the events of my childhood, I am still responsible for them. I find it refreshing to hear you blast those callers who refer to themselves as survivors, adult children of . . . I find those people to be offensive to those of us who truly are survivors; those of us who have overcome our adversities and worked hard to improve our circumstances. Once we decide to make the best of whatever our situation is, we will be better people and the world will be a much better place in which to live."

We have become a nation of excuses and victims. The inevitable defensive consequence of that thinking is a denigration of individuals who do well in spite of circumstances. I've been horrified at how many blacks who accomplish are dismissed as Uncle/Aunt Toms. I've been horrified at how many women who don't see the world as wholly a male conspiracy organized against them are dismissed as either ignorant or elite.

Understanding inequities and evils should motivate actions of rectification, but sugggesting that history is destiny and that individuals are created by their pasts is an insult to the capacity of human beings to overcome. The implication is that there is no individual responsibility to overcome. I think there is. Everyone must overcome something. That simply is life.

It has become politically correct never to hold anyone accountable for their circumstance and actions . . . mostly, I think, because advocates for each societal subgroup have legitimate claims about certain conditions and realities in society. But these subgroups inaccurately assume all their actions to be a response to those conditions (always the negative ones), never to a lack of character, courage, morality, values, life-style, and choices. Well, they are just wrong, wrong, wrong.

I want to paraphrase the words of Larry Elder, a black conservative talk-show host in Los Angeles, when speaking to a black woman who was complaining and blaming "whites": "Jews were practically annihilated during World War II, and have been continual targets throughout history. You don't see them doing drive-by shootings and killing their own babies, do you?" Hooray, and thank you.

This all brings to mind something I read twenty years ago: "Modesty is superiority bowing to mediocrity." Our society has actually made some people feel ashamed of rising above circumstance; they are regarded as undermining some "cause." This is a disaster for all of us. People who overcome problems should be our heros, not our targets, simply because their courageous actions underscore our own mediocrity.

PUFF THE MAGIC DRAGON

I'm likewise astonished that repetitive destructive behaviors are called "diseases" and "addictions." I can see some obvious benefits for doing so: physicians and therapists can use the "disease" classification number to charge insurance companies for treatment; and the onus for personal responsibility is removed—since you've been overcome by something out of your control, thereby relieving your guilt. Our culture definitely seeks to avoid all pain or discomfort, either physical or emotional or social.

Dear Dr. Laura:
    In these days of feelgood something-or-otherology, where "addiction" means, "I like it, so I'm not going to stop doing it," you have refused to allow

people to talk "addiction" or "dysfunctional" or blame their current difficulties on past abuses. You really should listen to some of the %&#@* that passes for insight on both radio and television. Your insistence that your callers take personal responsibility for their actions is tantamount to schism from much of what I have heard elsewhere.

Sincerely,
Philip

The current pop-psych therapy (and books and tapes) trend of alleviating most of all personal responsibility from the equation of behavioral choices is simply about making sure nobody feels bad (the ultimate anesthetic)—and that's what scares me. While compassion would seem to dictate that we work on relieving someone's pain as soon as possible, we forget not only that pain is very motivating, but also that guilt and shame are necessarily painful.

Acknowledging that you are basically the perpetrator of your mess of a life is admittedly very upsetting. But it is that very acknowledgment that gives you the power to change things. After all, what you can take away, you can give.

Keith, twenty-one, was on drugs for eight years. "I took anything. And I did anything to get them, including selling," he admitted freely.

"Keith, you did all the drugs because . . . ?"

"To have fun with my friends, it was a blast, I just liked it."

"Why aren't you on drugs anymore? Why give up the fun?"

"Hmmm . . . well, I had some long-range goals, and they just weren't panning out. I tried changing classes, jobs, friends, love relationships, etcetera, and still wasn't getting anywhere.

Then I realized that I was the constant in the equation, and the constant was that I was using drugs."

"Good for you, Keith. It was a decision to start using drugs. Another decision to continue doing them. And a final decision to stop."

"Yeah, that's right. But the reason I'm calling you today is I'm having a problem trying to feel love consistently . . . "

"Keith, we all want our feelings to be consistent. This includes feelings about self, life, others, choices. No can do . . . unless you're consistently drugged."

"Right, I see what you mean. When I was high, things were consistent . . . no that's not right . . . they just seemed that way. But in real life, yeah . . . Thank you, Dr. Laura."

While it is the end of Keith's drug use, it is only the beginning of his learning a more spiritual and realistic means of dealing with the inconsistencies and difficulties of real life.

Keith decided to confront a habit and lick it. He wasn't diseased. A friend of mine has diabetes and thyroid problems. These are diseases. These he can't stop, no matter how much honorable behavior he displays.

While the use of recreational drugs and alcohol can cause a disease state of various tissues and organs in the body, it is a disease of the will (determination to do what is right, healthy, and good), of character (acknowledging the negative impact you're having on others and not letting it continue), and of courage (sustaining yourself through the difficult part of beating a habit).

You can choose to try to lubricate yourself through life, skimming along on the top of a shallow pond, with food, drugs, sex, or you can choose to have a life of meaning, value, and goodness. The latter requires respect for this delicate, temporary entity you call your life.

I CHOOSE TO MAKE IT BE SO . . . AND IT WILL BE SO

How do we get by those times when positive feelings have hidden and negative feelings loom too large? You can choose to behave "as if" the good feelings were still there. It is actually a choice!

Jane got it:

> I moved five hundred miles away from home last year when I was eight months pregnant and with an active toddler. I left all my family and lifelong friends when my husband was transferred to his corporate office here. I was all for the move, excited about the change, but scared as well.
>
> After the initial excitement of the move and the birth of my baby, the stress and loneliness set in and I found myself becoming prone to periods of self-pity and had a few good pouts. Listening to your show shook me back to reality, helped me to pull myself together, accept responsibility for moving here by my own choice.
>
> You helped me to remember that if I act happy, I probably will be happy, and you were right.
>
> Now, a year later, my kids are happy, I have some new friends with young children in my neighborhood, we have started a new business which allows me to work in my home.
>
> It required some work and personal honesty on my part, but I thank you for giving me the ideas and thoughts and kick in the pants I needed to get started.

What a radical idea: choosing how to behave regardless of how you feel—and discovering that behaving differently seems to change how you feel. So much for feelings being the irrefutable truth when you assess a situation.

A quote sent to me by Sam and Brenda fits in right here: "Sometimes it seems like you can't change anything. Sometimes by changing yourself you change everything."

This is true even in less than ideal situations, where people choose to honor past commitments and obligations even though they wouldn't choose those today.

A listener wrote:

> I know I have made many stupid decisions in my life. My parents always ask me, "What happened? You were the one who was supposed to succeed with all your A's in school!" I now understand that making A's in school doesn't mean that you are smart in other ways. So many times I hear you say that a teenager is not capable of picking a life mate and you are so right. My husband is not an evil man, but he would not be my choice today. I know my mistakes but do not know where to go from here except to learn from them, to grow, and to teach my children about love, self-respect, education, and setting goals and reaching them.

It is at this crucial point, where things aren't exactly the way we hoped they'd be, and we aren't as happy as we imagined we'd be, that we often make the biggest mistakes, sacrificing deeply rooted principles for a thrill. Jane dealt with that dilemma with honor and maturity. Now what about Steve?

THIS IS TODAY? . . . I'LL PICK YESTERDAY

Steve, forty-five, had a girlfriend when he was eighteen, but her parents objected to "young love."

"I ended up marrying another wonderful woman and have had twenty-six years of a wonderful marriage with two great children."

"So far, Steve, you sound like a fortunate fellow."

"Yeah, I am . . . I know it. Anyway, I recently found out that she has never married. And I have been thinking about her a lot. I've been thinking of, you know, getting in touch with her . . . "

"Wait a minute, hold on! Steve, have you considered that her never marrying might be a red flag? Are you honestly fantasizing that she's not married because she's been waiting for you for over twenty years?"

"Well, no . . . not really . . . yeah maybe . . . "

"Steve, are you contemplating a choice between that lost love and your wonderful marriage?"

"Umm, maybe . . . yes, I have thought about it."

"You know what, Steve? This is the stuff movie fantasy is made of, and in that venue it usually works out okay. But in this world you would devastate your wife and children and extended family, dishonor all the respect and consideration given you for a quarter of a century, lose the family connectedness and security, and the only thing on the other side is a 'what if.' Are you really prepared to lose all that just to recapture an adolescent dream?"

"I don't know. It doesn't seem right . . . does it?"

"You are looking to a fairy tale to rejuvenate your life. Why don't you be your own Merlin and do what it takes to bring magic back into making your life wonderful."

"That's why I called you, Dr. Laura. I was hoping you'd

help me get my head back on straight. Thank you."

Somehow too many people have gotten the notion that their immediate gratification and final tally of life's experiences is sacred above all other considerations, obligations, commitments, and vows. This thinking destroys individuals, families, and societies. Look around you. It's happening.

OH THE TANGLED WEB WE WEAVE

I've gotten the impression from so many callers that decisions are mostly based on the feelings and expediency of the moment—a moment that passes long before it can even be fully contemplated. We decide in the "now" and live in the "forever after."

"Live for today," is the cheer of those who seem to rely on tomorrow never coming. Decisions are best made with consideration of the most probable consequences; instead I hear, "I never thought much about it," or "I just hoped it would work itself out."

Bernadette, twenty-four, has been shacking up with a fellow for four months. She has just found out that his ex-girl-friend is two months pregnant (is that what you call "ex"?). Brace yourself: so is Bernadette. Bernadette left this bloke when she found out about the dueling pregnancies, but has recently learned that the other girl is out of the picture (didn't we already think that once before?). She is calling about making the decision to go back to him or not.

"When you're pregnant, your emotions and thinking are indeed challenged. But, Bernadette, how can you imagine thinking the problem is solved because the other girl is out of the picture? The other girl was never the problem—your live-in stud's dishonorable character is."

When I questioned Bernadette on the good sense of going back, she kept coming at me with "I thought/hoped/feel . . ." statements that unfortunately speak more to her fantasies than her realities. Oh, if hoping and wishing had power.

"Bernadette," I continued, "your initial decision to move in with him and be sexually active, apparently without contraception, did not, as you secretly hoped, mean you were in a stable, healthy, committed relationship. You were practicing alchemy if you thought so."

"Oh, this is all so difficult to accept . . . "

"Bernadette, you've got to accept it—for the sake of your child. Failed alchemy got you here, and false hopefulness will only get your deeper."

Bernadette needed to acknowledge and accept her gross mistakes and finally take some responsibility. I suggested adoption so that the child would have a mature, intact, committed, two-parent family. We could have spent our time understanding how past hurts and low-self esteem drove her to these self-defeating behaviors, which is always interesting and sometimes instructive. Nonetheless, I thought it was more important to attempt to engage her good sense—show her that self-esteem and a better life come from making tough decisions, suffering through loss and growth, and ennobling herself through compassion for the predicament of someone else; in this case, an unborn child.

FACE IT, YOU'RE JUST NOT YOUR BEST SELF YET

I had an interesting call just the other day that fits right into this discussion of how decisions set the scene, and in so doing, come to define the drama that is your life.

Kurt, twenty-three, is supposed to be getting married in a few months, and called about the problem he was having with his best friend, who is to be a groomsman. It seems his friend is mad at him about something that occurred last weekend. They were in a bar together having drinks and after the usual too many, Kurt started kissing, necking, and petting with some woman. His friend is furious at him and refuses to stand by him at the wedding unless he tells his fiancée.

"Dr. Laura," he asked me, "what should I do?"

"Frankly, Kurt, it sounds to me that you have a drinking problem and are nowhere near developed enough to respect the meaning of commitment and love."

"You could be right . . . "

"But in answer to your question, I strongly suggest you tell your fiancée about the situation. She deserves the dignity of knowing the truth. You also ought to cut down or eliminate your drinking, and you and your fiancée should go into at least three months of premarital counseling. Above all, you should thank your friend for being a real friend, and if it becomes necessary, postpone the wedding."

"But what about the expense of calling it off?"

"What about the expense of hurt feelings and the possible termination of a relationship? That night at the bar you made a choice, and it was a bad one. I just want to reiterate how much your friend must care about you to risk making you face very important and uncomfortable, if not ugly, truths."

I think Kurt got the message of how, in turn, he must be caring toward his fiancée by telling her the awful truth.

After my conversation with Kurt, I got this anonymous fax:

On today's show you had a caller who had a problem because one of his groomsmen wants out of

his wedding party. I think he left the call realizing how good a friend he had and that the right thing to do would be to postpone the wedding. But, he seemed utterly trapped by the financial loss required.

What's money when we are talking about a life-long commitment to a woman who will be the mother of his children? If it were his fiancée with the problem would he want to marry her and let things just magically take care of themselves later? So he loses some down payments here and there. He'll be saving himself a bundle later in marriage counseling or lawyer's fees.

I married with problems with fidelity and I ended up hurting someone very special in a way I can never make up for. There's a lot of embarrassment with calling off a wedding. I've seen it happen, but it can't compare with the hurt of a promise never meant. Treat your word like diamonds and others will hold on to them as such. Sometimes you'll find that's all you have to give.

PITY BUT NOT PARDON

And when you've been on the receiving end of someone's lack of character, courage, or conscience, what of your decision to excuse or forgive? One of the more frequent types of calls to my radio program is about being wronged and deciding whether or not to stay with that person, and/or forgive them after they've wronged you.

Forgiving and staying don't have to go hand in hand. Forgiving has more to do with a letting go of the intensity of emotion that is a reaction to the dastardly deeds. Forgiving is about putting events in perspective and getting on. Forgiving does not demand acceptance.

Some folks want to get on with forgiving simply to stay connected because being on their own looms too large. The trouble they often have is that they realize that some things ought not be pardoned.

Kathy, twenty-nine, has had a three-year relationship with a "wonderful guy." They are engaged. When a job promotion required her going briefly out of town for some training, he got "lonely" and had a sexual fling with someone else. It's been four months since Kathy found out.

"Should I stay with him?" she asked, plaintively.

Well, let's examine the situation. If someone does something as an "event" rather than as an ongoing behavior, and they experience deep guilt and remorse, is the person profoundly changed by the experience? In that situation, something is gained, albeit at someone else's expense. If a person assumes full responsibility for their actions and make efforts to redress, then something is gained.

However, sometimes even events can clue you into character faults and weaknesses that may need a lot of time to evolve into a higher state of being . . . sometimes too much time.

In Kathy's case, did her promotion threaten her boyfriend? Did he use sex to even things up or make himself feel more powerful? Is he incapable of being alone and containing lustful feelings even for a few days? If that is so, how will he deal with threats to his narcissism given the eventual ennui and difficulties of an ongoing marriage and life?

I advised Kathy to take a few years to determine all of the above, because her fiancé put himself in a very high-risk category by his decisions to lick his wounds instead of honoring his word.

Kathy then needs to decide if, in the context of all his past behaviors, it is worth staying with him and investing in his "evolution." Sometimes, though, an honest assessment of the past shows us that small weeds have been in this garden a long time—weeds we frantically pluck out so the garden will appear clean.

Kathy's decision could go either way, as long as her eyes are wide open. Some situations are clearer, but no less painful.

LIKE IT OR LUMP IT

Sue, thirty, has an agonizing decision to make. Her alcholic mother is extremely disruptive and destructive. Sue has told her mother that she will no longer see her unless she gets off the booze, and/or goes into some serious program to help herself.

Sue's problem? Her brother and father have gone after her with a vengeance, telling her she is mean, destroying the family, and that she is exaggerating Mom's problem.

Sue is mired in self-doubt. She feels she didn't give her mother this edict as an ultimatum, but rather to release herself from having to confront the denials and the destructiveness of the relationship with her mother. She's wondering if she's right or has the right to do what she's done.

In our conversation it became clear that Sue's pain was not guilt from having done her mom wrong; the pain was her mourning, finally, the loss of her mother. This was the ultimate insult of her mother's choice to drink for the sake of her own feelings; she robs others of a wife, mother, and friend and makes their announcement of pain an act of selfishness. Wow, if this isn't getting things backward!

We as a society have gotten turned around on this aspect.

We've become like little children refusing to take fault or responsibility for doing what we damn well want to do. We say we can't help ourselves, that the other person is being judgmental and lacks understanding. We say that until the pile of poop under us gets too high—then we move, all right.

TO BE OR NOT TO BE MORAL

Everything you do is by conscious choice. Choices are between options. All options are not equal in their potential outcomes, much less inherent value.

I had an on-air discussion with a fellow who was concerned about the rightness or wrongness of something he did, based upon the outcome. He was actually suggesting that the rightness or wrongness of something is only judged after the fact: if the result wasn't what you hoped . . . oops . . . guess that was a bad thing. So, rape is only bad if the woman gets upset or pregnant? Stealing is only bad if it's from someone poor?

He never did seem to get what I meant.

One woman, with a valued marriage and family, wondered if her affair was never found out, would it still be wrong? After all, if no one knows, it doesn't hurt anybody. But the potential for hurt is always there, isn't it?

A follow-up fax from Eussa:

> I just heard the caller wondering whether or not it would be right for her to fool around with a long-time business acquaintance since no one would know. My husband and his employee started their relationship by commuting together to clients', bowling during lunches, racquetball after work, and having "business" lunches. Now they are living together while still

getting their respective divorces. We even went on a skiing vacation together with our spouses. I objected and felt threatened by their relationship, but I was told that I was unreasonable, nothing was happening and I ought to be able to handle their relationship without irrational jealousy.

I am alone raising four, very young children. I am also trying to forgive my husband, because I know it is best for me in order to move on, although it is damn hard!

One measure I give to reinforce the general conscience of the listening audience is this: "Would you want this act open to public scrutiny? If the answer is no, then no amount of rationalization is going to purify it."

In making decisions here are some rules, freely paraphrased from "The Morals of Chess," written in 1779 by Benjamin Franklin:

1. Foresight: Look into the future and consider the consequences. Think about the real advantages to yourself, then wonder about the impact on others and how that might then reflect back on your life. Imagine how you might righteously defend your position.
2. Circumspection: Examine the bigger picture, the dangers, the possibilities, the probabilities. Be more brave about options that scare you.
3. Caution: Don't make moves in haste or in passion. Keep to the rules and guidelines of etiquette, law, and Commandments. And, understand that once you've made your move, you set into play a series of events over which you may not have recourse, from which you might suffer in your soul, as well as your life.

IS THERE A RIVER OF NO RETURN?

And what if you've blown the above?

From an anonymous letter: "How do you get over hating yourself for something you have done wrong that was against your morals?"

Well, if it is truly guilt and not just a sadness that it's all gone bad 'cause you've gotten caught, the first thing you must realize is that only good people feel guilt. And then good people do good things with the gained knowledge.

As one mother wrote me:

> I know that I am a wonderful mother and could and will learn how to be even better. But I wasn't always a wonderful mother, and I think it was a critical point for my child where I should've been—and now he may be paying the price for that for the rest of his life.
>
> I know I can't redo the past, but this is tough to accept and tougher to live with. Today I am very involved with his life, which requires "special needs," and I make much better decisions for us. I've learned to respect myself and know there's a lot I need to do and learn.
>
> But this does not dissolve my mistakes or make the guilt that's with them go away. He is my life and if I do anything to hurt him intentially or not, I tear up.

Acknowledgement, true remorse, change, and redress are what we have available; a commitment to a life of character, courage, and conscience and the motivation to teach others. Perhaps the lingering guilt is there lest we forget.

⋆   ⋆   ⋆

This chapter is all about the ultimate truth of your freedom. No matter the stimulus (fear, lust, need, historical hurts), your response is not predetermined (escape, mate, take, perpetually suffer): you ultimately choose. You can choose to react like a one-celled amoeba, strictly determined to avoid all discomfort. Or, you can choose to react like a human being, with the ability to make choices, acknowledging that the absense of hurt and discomfort is insufficient to give your life meaning or purpose.

Death. Uncertainty. Loss. Tragedy. Threat. Conflict. Aloneness. Rejection. Those, to use a mathematical term, are "givens" in life. When one or more of them "happens," it's not a punishment or a curse or bad luck. You haven't been cosmically selected—it's simply that you're experiencing one of the many components of life; in the way rotted organic material is a part of the soil in which plants grow and flourish.

Therefore, it is not the absence of such challenges that makes life pleasurable or meaningful. It is the choices you make in your reactions to deal with them that determine the quality of your life. Most of the time you don't get to select your challenges; sometimes your challenges are the direct consequences of previous choosing. You may not even like any of the available options. However, you never lose the freedom and responsibility to choose and then honor that choice.

When these choices are determined by virtue and values, you bring purpose, meaning, and integrity to your life. When your choices are determined by amoebic instinct . . .

Postscript

⁓

The concept of maintaining personal integrity even in the face of external insult, disappointment, rejection, or hurt is even dealt with in the Bible (Genesis 4:6–7, Tanakh) as God, after giving "positive feedback" only to Abel and his offering and noticing Cain's upset reaction, says to Cain:

> Why are you so distressed,
> And why is your face fallen?
> Surely if you do right,
> There is an uplift.
> But if you do not do right
> Sin couches at the door;
> Its urge is toward you,
> Yet you can be its master.

It seems to me that God is teaching us that joy comes from doing "right," in spite of the reaction from or input by others, including God. God also reassures us that we do have the capacity to rise above circumstance and attain mastery over our weaker selves, attaining the nobility that has become *human* beings.

Dr. Laura Schlessinger, forty-eight, is married to Dr. Lew Bishop and lives in Southern California with her son, Deryk, ten.

Dr. Schlessinger received her Ph.D. in Physiology from Columbia University in New York. She earned her Post-Doctoral Certification in Marriage and Family Therapy from USC. She is licensed in California as a Marriage and Family Counselor.

Her radio program, *The Laura Schlessinger Show,* is syndicated internationally; she is one of the most listened to talk-show hosts in North America.

Dr. Schlessinger holds a black belt in Hapkido Karate, is a "bad" Trekkie, collects unique teapots, loves powerboating and bike riding, and is an avid reader of mysteries and books on Jewish thinking.